Kelvin Corcoran

Other Books by Kelvin Corcoran:-

Robin Hood in the Dark Ages
The Red and Yellow Book
Qiryat Sepher
TCL
The Next Wave
Lyric Lyric
Melanie's Book
When Suzy Was
Your Thinking Tracts or Nations

Kelvin Corcoran

New and Selected Poems

Shearsman Books
2004

First published in the United Kingdom in 2004 by
Shearsman Books
58 Velwell Road
Exeter EX4 4LD

http://www.shearsman.com/

ISBN 0-907562-39-9

The four illustrations in the section *from Your Thinking Tracts or Nations* are all
by Alan Halsey, and are copyright © Alan Halsey, 2001. They are reproduced here
by kind permission of the artist and of West House Books, Sheffield, publishers of
Your Thinking Tracts or Nations.

Cover illustrations:

Photograph of a painted wooden ceiling in George Mavros' house, Ambelakia, by
Melanie Warnes, copyright © Melanie Warnes, 2004. Rear cover photograph of the
author by Melanie Warnes, copyright © Melanie Warnes, 2004.

Acknowledgements:

My Life With Byron is published with agreement from Rod Mengham of Equipage,
to whom thanks are due. Parts of *My Life With Byron* appeared in earlier forms
in *Oasis*.

Poems from *Against Purity* have been published in *Oasis* (edited by Ian Robinson),
Shearsman (edited by Tony Frazer), *Great Works* (edited by Peter Philpott),
Crossing the Line, a first anthology from the reading series (selected by David
Miller) in *Painted, spoken, no. 6*, *GutCult – A West House Anthology* (edited by
Alan Halsey) and *kultureflash* edited by Barry Schwabsky).

Contents

from **When Suzy Was** (1999)

from **Melanie's Book** (1996)

from **Lyric Lyric** (1993)

from **The Next Wave** (1990)

Against Purity

(New Poems, 2004)

Ino

By the well of Thalami, Ino my bride,
come out of your house, come out in the night,
with ship gods as well as land gods,
with bronze statues on the island
in the open air of Pephnos,
with the whiter than usual ants.

The owls swoop down
on dark wires sure as death,
hunting in pairs, back and forth
threading the night.

My mind empties around the tower
of Kapetanios Christeas and into the sea;
my old neighbour sings at night,
her imperfect beautiful voice
rises for no-one or the moon, Ino, for no-one,
or the dark ocean wrapped around the world.

Myriorama

By the houses of the living
and the houses of the dead
congregation of flames burn.

A door opened in the ground
releases the great blackness,
first light unfurled the sky.

Keeper of the chambered sea,
they say that in the sea . . .
the story is widespread.

Details vary along the coast,
but the baby Ino, was a god?
– out of a box from the sea.

                    *

Under the bronze mountains spring walks,
girls follow in translation
one moment in the garden tracing Lusieri.

Blinds make bars across the page,
errant note? No, I remember the bliss
of the lines, my eyes opening on them.

Byron's estates in Eng-a-land
annexed to the big idea,
[exeunt the peasantry through every possible landscape]

I cast the cards of the myriorama
for musing swains and lacustrine vistas,
traffic jams and haunted bedrooms.

Turner asking Elgin for £400 p.a.
– I have been obliged to be a little barbarous –
and the Cretan fish eating all Lusieri's pictures.

Ten men line up to shoot Judas for Easter,
Nicolo dancing on the ruins of empire,
Nicolo dancing on broken stones and harbours.

Yannis Ritsos is free.

*

As we came out of the mountains
the moment not day or night,
music surrounded us.

Out of the silence of the gorge
through walls of rock and air,
we walked in a tunnel of sound.

Long-song synthesised unearthly,
swirl of sea and Taygetos
shatters into goat bells.

Reforms into music of the passes,
random harmonics, goat stink
rises up to us earth song replete.

*

This is Radio Free Byron on the short wave
broadcasting to the English shires: wake up.
We urge war against the west, against Fletcher;
the Maniots are the men for me, they will do the deed.

Wake up you boys and girls, you sneak careerists,
forget the English Bores co-option of Ashbery,
the discontinuous prose continues;
this is the big poem of right belief – immaculate.

That black speck veering across your sky space
above the town where you live,
riding cold fronts off the map,
homing in, set at zero, is your death.

With this magnifying glass in both hands
I burn sunspots on the calendar,
burn for canonic, burn for garland on your head,
so each day comes up fresh with a hole in it.

*

Running the high meadows
day and night in the skin of a lynx
the bloody meniscus sticks.

Swallows roll in mountain air,
pop music, something emotional, defiant,
reaches into the same blue quarter.

Yannis Ritsos is free.

A Shelley Poet

12 July 1822 from the harbour Agios Dimitrios

Calm languid sea on every side
the air as though resting above
one fishing boat
               sails out of the gulf
leaving a long, subtle wake.

                    *

and then nothing

the same etc sleep

                    *

at night a boat came in
battered, sails gone
from another world by the looks,
the Ariel
two men and a boy

                    *

They came ashore next morning
and greeted Kapetanios Christeas.
They are a Shelley poet,
Cpt Williams and a boy Vivian,
the Shelley recites Sophocles
and revolution very excited,
(we have it here already)

saying life of triumph and
something after a big storm.
The Shelley jumps about like a boy,
Christeas looks at him puzzled
in the great morning of the world.

*

He read Hellas to us, we sat around the tower,
he looks at us and says the final chorus was right,
the rest was bluster rhetoric with something about our fig tree
– which was not his to give for it anyway.
Christeas liked the fighting parts
and made the shouts of victory victory.

The Shelley dug his hands into the red soil
and held the white rocks in the shade of mimosa,
he looks at the sea everyday and will not leave.

The Shelley in earth twisting and turning,
came out from under that language
unblinking to get it right.

Empires crack
              the snake renews itself
green and mighty spring returns.

The sea made noise all night,
mountains of water falling on the harbour;
I went to look in the morning,
the confused messages flooding the horizon
and the light changing depth,

Here we sit like birds in the wilderness.

*

I am alive on Cape Sublime,
the sea and mountains blend in song
this place was once called Pephnos

Around the tower and into the deep,
mistress of many voices
walked into the water

Out of the shining I saw her then
keeper of the chambered sea,
white goddess who saved me

Here there is no shadow
in the sky, no authority
rising to dull the lens of light

here I am, this way boy,
swim to me, into my arms

Season of Broken Doors

between Ag. Nic and Ag. Dim
near the dry river bed

above Kalamata to?
small white
J quotes coke, Krischios outside

road to Neohori – 2
old rusty and new deluxe

between Saidona and Kastania
white cross black cross photo

road out of K
cross on top, after Exohori sign

as 6 Ag. Bapbapa

30/3 between Argos and Tripoli
the mountain road, no toll
white flowers everywhere

*

I found boxes scattered along the roads,
secret, earthbound constellations;
their contents would make Cornell blush
weathering into a new coherence.

*

Jesus quotes coke
by the river bed Salinitsa,
a fusebox burning.

The sides are rusty
– stick your tongue on it,
taste salt, lemon, blood.

This machine of objects
blooms tectonic
on the fault of right belief.

At the end of exile
you open the door and
the circuit of air ignites.

*

My family home stands above the western portal,
the one gate of Monemvasia; my obviously heroic head
stares at empty sea-lanes striking liars dumb.

I look at weeds, trinkets, strangers,
passing into the erosion I feel; if one word escaped
I would shatter in a new diaspora.

But listen you stones, you politicians:
Yannis Ritsos is free.

Singing Head

            Bodies of a man and child
off Lesvos, earlier in the same channel
three young girls.

No Sappho
No Aeschylus
No singing head afloat.

Afghan banknotes in their pockets,
they are thrown overboard or the boats sink;
they cannot swim and the lifejackets fail,
some have never seen the sea before.

No Sappho
No Aeschylus
No singing head afloat.

Helen

Yannis told us of the alternative escape route,
Helen and Paris making chariot wheel tracks in Thalami
down to the harbour at Pephnos.

Spartans left waiting at Kranai,
mouths open, bored before the myth
– look at those sparks, like stars eh?

They spent their first night here,
fell upon one another, spent
until the sun came over Taygetos.

Helen set foot on board, trumpets sound
over water, sewing in the grain
the ships of all the world in her wake.

From the Harbour

We spring out of the box of winter,
that curling cloud, a letter – Chalcolithic,
that girl leaning towards you,
that shadow in your cup – is from my hand.

I wait at the door to your house, ivy tattooing the wall,
spurge blooms on the hill behind me;
I swept down from Thrace and the narrow pass
from blueprint villages in Anatolia to this warm water port.

Where is my sister now?
the light in slices shot through your thinking dark,
and the sky cracking over the whole world.
My sister? – trumpets calling from the water.

I swept down, my birds in random green go mad,
on to this landing strip between mountain and sea,
into this natural amphitheatre
I set my foot for riot to follow.

The ground returns my tread, the chambered earth,
and she steps ashore.

*

I found a plastic bull on the beach,
toy Zeus fronting the waves erect
with bleached hide and shrivelled horn
– if he grins girls, you're over his back
crashing towards a bed of luxury, where it all begins.

He has the look of you about him Byron,
the set of his head and lordly gaze,
though I forget we are both dead
I think you would like him,
he bellows sweet amphionic odes.

Let's walk him along the cape,
spring begins again with his snort;
we danced all our lives to his delicate step,
to the beat of his blood, even now
as old as we are, descending in shadows.

Yours, Shiloh

*

Those stories, those songs were television to us
except alive on air they wrapped us in their signal,
except that we ran it and it was real
in the grain of the wave as we cleared the harbour.

So, like birds in the wilderness, we are its variations,
making the picture atomised, the republic of light,
and the sea shaping a tunnel of sound
as long and slow as summer around the western shore.

*

After his victory at Actium Octavius founded Nicopolis,
a blighted shithole befitting his political soul:
call him Blair, Bush, Sharon or Milošević,
those who are wired to the world, who cannot set ambition aside.

23

Of Antony an old man said, he was glued to her,
a lover's soul lives in the body of his mistress
and she set sail for the Peloponnesus;
off Taenarus her women reunited them.

They spoke and afterwards did sup and lie together;
across the dark calm of the sea Antony said,
– we are keeping company with famous ghosts,
Helen and Paris sailed this way to their final sortie.

Let's glide to the cave below the headland
and paddle in the mouth of hell, hand in hand
we'll walk the streets of our burning city
and gather the asphodel of our sweet defeat.

                    *

Stack the myriorama vertically,
each card suspended apart
a spatial landscape made temporal,
olive tree blown white in the wind.

Seeds, insects crowd the air,
oil from the boatyard bleeds into concrete,
at night Kurds come ashore
we turn them round if we can.

The walls flake into the sea,
palimpsest, underwriter
of this harbour between worlds
opening its broken arms.

The Empire Stores

A reading of Alan Halsey's *Dante's Barber Shop*
                    (De Vulgari Eloquentia)

'How can we sing King Alpha's song in a strange land?'
                    (The Melodians)

1

We closed down the Empire Stores in the bay,
we don't shop there now, only for our imaging
of the map of others and zero longitude fancy,
globally patched, then a rising tide at your door.

Or the ineluctable, brimful culture piled up
lettering every street, heaps of incoming names,
and even this is not my thinking,
see all this dirt fair clogs my eyes.

Be clear: we reject the old but new holy war,
the demographics of canonic fodder, new but old flags
– these colours don't fade;
give me rivers of dirt and bring my poets back to life.

It's those conversations I want, you speak
Oh England on slick rails to the dumb chamber;
put your ear to the ground, your hands in the air,
there's a chance archival unity won't rise and shine you.

If what follows is a metaphor then this is no poem
– Caspian oil sucked across the Stans to Karachi;
it's not a silvery zero tube but ignition:
make the ordinary language good or die.

2

With grammar stocks rising on song
he sat opposite me at the big event;
– cosy up to them and push their hot buttons,
triangulate the Blairprint and common thought.

When Shelley arrived out of the ever living past
he checked in at the King Otto, Byron next door;
he saw dark figures rise before the liberals,
how the few valued the many and bought the government.

They dribbled conscience on the accounts,
we stare at the glaze mostly, eyes glued to the past
cold filtered through a grovel image voodoo,
clean up and apply to Concept House.

What scene unfolds in that domed snow shaker?
White boys on the road, zoot suits and patronage,
a limited view of human nature
in a medium of implacable pessimism.

To make us the object of such devotion
the secret voice print is calling,
in rank order, men, women, family groups,
our faces tipped into the light and locked.

3

If we could write an archaeology of the soul,
unable to speak in a barcode dancing,
the little birdies would sing for St. Valentine
with big light raining on a Vatican elsewhere.

But we came dark cloud boiling from white north
drawn by the smell of luxury goods;
the journey knocked narrative out of our poetry,
even pedants see it vanish as lives unravel.

See the red, the golden threads tied in secret knots,
slipped from your pommel into Scythian scrub;
the religious spillage in our wake is trash:
what other authority do you dream?

Such ingenuity we had kept those ships afloat,
allowed our parents to eat in that war;
she said learning English would make her free
and the perfect sentence dismantled Ilium.

To begin again, the girls coming and going
set their feet in the meadow,
in the red, the golden day, the invention of fair writing
in the meadow by the sea.

4

One day the secrets of the present war will be out,
– let's have a positive idea on the topic Capitano,
I'm ready, I'm taking down the boss words,
I is dredging it up the homeland tunnel.

Give me the spoken order like balm in the air.
Give me the holy father dumb in Gilead.
Give me trade ban and big starey eyed kids.
Give me a cypher on two legs, clueless.

Anything but watching it live on t.v.
It's not a cure for pain, that day, that morphine song,
you already know the colours, the palm tree cutouts,
sound off, text up – in B ghd t d y.

Talk to this wooden face, Marydoll, prissy lips,
they have tunnels under the desert, intricate and rich;
awaiting glory elevated in the sky garden,
the poverty of public discourse goes unsaid.

Who wrote the history of truth telling? What's the ratio?
Without Shelley, MacSweeney and little TC?
Ye boys of England, from the midlands and the north,
clean up the abattoirs and each chartered grave.

5

Jerusalem the Golden shipped up in the south east,
in the Valley of Dawn they believe what they like;
see the mansions on the hills, barred and empty
– last time I looked, the variable script disintegrated.

We made deep pools of all our anxieties,
hungry mouth at the bottom of the well said nought;
plans for the real world in the language of beasts,
a distilled purity, contra natura, abhorrent.

Come dance with me Joanna, Ioanna Southcott,
Ioanna big mouth, the sun is always rising
in the riff riff valley of Don Van Vliet,
I was miles away myself, under a sky thick with migrating souls.

Do you think for one minute this dub dub over tracking
out of the ever living past très moderne?
Wake up, the room is full; Shelley and Ric and young MacSweeney,
dying for want of intelligent talk.

And what will happen to any of us?
Speechless boy of a speechless tribe,
see the nation of morning, nation of supple creatures
beneath the pretty page of a kind empire.

6

Shelley took wing, wrapped up Lundy Fastnet,
sent thought balloons across the Bristol Channel
to the slave trade capital, a power of no good,
astride its Palladian funding stream.

He was my aerial in that broadcast
on the ever living short wave, anagrammatical;
court historians swing on the rim of the imperium,
snorting stipends, vamping up the Empire News.

Our Boys March Along Candlelit Streets
Babylon Falls To The West – Byblos Taken
Child Prostitutes Lie Down In Alleyways
Make A New Home In King Alpha's Land

Shelley took wing on that day,
migratory birds homing in joined the dots;
in one moment radar spelt it out,
the lost art of traffic control, welfare, moderation.

I was miles away myself and rushing back,
at the same time the pigeons of Assuit rise
and the white wings of our common books open
lifting into the crowded light one word.

Against Purity

Out of sight at the boundary
blue hills and magical trees
mock and dance in around,
the greater life flashing in the sky.

Somewhere believe or singing her
a field god rises, hungry,
close to the ground, eyes like smoke,
singing her those particles wake.

They say that they say that sometimes
she's seen in the neighbourhood.

*

I see things out in the fields,
the word heliotrope in blood;
in the faces of our children
the road's a dark river.

I see things in the other room,
Melanie's dream speaking
the old women click clack,
blind in a circle oblivious.

They say that they say
she forced her way into the room,
she broke the circle, slit the cloth
of the empty air where the dead spin round.

Common Measure

Lifted away on England's heat wave
into an earlier dawn rising over Asia;
imagine a city as micro-circuit,
the whiz and pop of hot lights and money.

I remember common measure, 4/3 4/3 or 8/6,
how Burns shapes the stanza's second part,
the emerging truth where everything fits
rushing past us both, my fair, my lovely charmer.

The lights of Moscow cartwheel and further east
the dust of lights descending;
the business will go elsewhere,
across the world turned upside down.

4/3 4/3 or 8/6, common measure
sings up from every street on Earth.

*

On the top of this column
the English peck at the pool, float, make plans;
the sky sweats, ripped red over Kowloon
with a line from W.S. Graham in Argyle Street:
We. Know. Nothing. About. These. Lives.

The boy made good into a ghost
sleeps on cardboard at the ferry terminal,
a bottle of water at his head;
he's released from the metaphor
in red and gold script, not exactly pictures.

The island night spangles names
bouncing over the South China Sea,
workmen shout, sink steel pillars in mud;
a market opens its mouth: big teeth, big hunger.

My students amend their texts in Cantonese:
juxtaposition   copse   pump room.

*

They cross the river from the mainland,
flower sellers, contract killers
to Macau of the casinos
in the morning of the world.

Our driver today is Alan
– the Republic there, the new causeway,
low camouflage hills
under abstractions of poured concrete.

We see the bones of the Japanese saints,
Xavier's scapula, teeth etc
on red cushions in cases,
to be returned to Hiroshima.

Asia is lit up and shopping.
Who knows what will happen?
The big names sparkle;
made in China, made in U.S.A.

Rowing across on the morning
flower laden boats, drawn up on this side.

MacSweeney

Here's a jar of honey for you;
we stand the beehives in the fields of borage,
the pollen's rich, the yields are high
from the bright blue flowers you knew.

Morning light spreads across the floor
despite liars in public places,
lapis miners get to work in Badaskhan
and wind lifts the ivy on the wall.

I walked out into the street,
we all moved together in a film;
faces lit from below, easily engaged,
and the blue Autumn sky falling away.

As if we said forever, buildings rise in air,
lives going in and out of them
and that would be above ground,
my girls growing up for instance.

The valley of the assassins has been extended
and escaped our rhetoric;
I'll pour the honey in the ground,
you rise up and spit the pearls in their faces.

The pollen's rich, the yields are high
from the bright blue flowers you knew.

Melanie I've been thinking about when we first met. How in all that trauma to ourselves and others, you would feed me the best soup, the best scrambled eggs, and then send me away. You were thinking what to do I think.

My obsession with you began then; each part, each limb, your mouth, your skin – each part of you, and you wanted to be wrapped around me entirely; an impossible hunger we couldn't understand and had never known before.

Mighty and literal, love burns the world to leave only your face above me in the dark room. I didn't know what was happening; driving back and forth by hidden reference points, flares in a sea reduced to one day, uncharted. Your face, my eyes on your face.

MIROLOYI *for Doug Oliver*

I saw Doug Oliver last night
standing in the shadow of the tower,
Christeas's tower guarding the harbour.

He was not in line at the ditch
and did not need to drink,
he was listening attentive, invisible.

The black sea filled his eyes,
he walked with Shelley unconfined
along the sea lanes of perfect sound.

He turned his good ear to the waveform;
his words, his maps and theories of song
released on the air unencumbered.

I heard the dialogue with Alice begin,
a woman came into the room a woman
back and forth flooding the paths under the sea.

I heard it all for the first time,
pretty weeds streamed from their hands,
bodies in sea light walking in one another.

                              *

And sucked down into the oracle of the drowned,
into the dry cave, back-lit psychorama and honey glow,
the echoed rise and fall of the waves
beats this moment and the next to the breathing of the sea;

he stands on the dry powder floor of this cave,
Peak district manifold, Apollonian on this shore.

But the dead can speak only through us,
around here the living feed the grave,
talk, share food and pour out their hearts
unblinking with love in the mortal fact,
the secret monologue broadcast,
I'm talking to my mother though 18 years dead.

So if I wait for Doug to speak, my teacher, my poet,
I imagine I'll wait for ever,
even in this dry cave, in honey light,
wrapped in the murmur of the sea, of bees;
in the honeycombed tunnels running to Matepan,
you hear Doug speak in a land made unstrange.

*

Look the owls swoop and dive from the tower for you,
alive in their dialogue of death;
I was thinking Alice of the life shared
and the lamentation of its ending,
their flight sounding in your ear, patterned and lethal,
their beautiful trajectories alight
against the black wall of mountain darkness.
Poetry is the way we think and speak here;
in one moment wing-beat instants take flight
over the gulf under the eyes of the serene empire,
to Methoni and Coroni in the darkening west
and the unpeopled cities of the sea.

FOUR MONOLOGUES

Leukothia

I am Leukothia, goddess of calm waters,
from the depths I watch the chambers of the sea;
I am companion to Poseidon,
call me mistress of good voyaging.

In my mortal story I was Ino,
daughter of Cadmus, lover then wife of Athamas,
sister of Semele the mother of Dionysus;
my other sister dismembered the fool Pentheus.

I saved the boy god, dressed the darling as a girl;
Hera drove me to madness and death for it and
my perfect dive into those arms,
in that world I breathe water.

Now I speak truth in dreams from the well,
the dark well-house of Thalami;
whatever the villagers ask is revealed,
a wet hole in the earth speaking.

In the spring they carry me out to their fields;
they ripple and wave for me,
men tightening sinews in my name;
they honour with me with their blood and fucking.

They say of me, they say of me
but who is speaking, do you think,
out of the well's dark mouth?
Even their dreams echo my voice.

But I long for the earth, the waving corn,
the boy god of my village standing up;
then in one moment the wave rises
turning limbs in vaulted light.

*

So I do what I can to save them,
they come from Albania, Iraq, India;
they walk, hide in containers and small boats.
I save them if I can, thinking of the voyage;
they come from Romania, Afghanistan, Iran;
from darkness to darkness, I lift them up.

They are not the first to journey this way,
I remember the Pelasgian and the Minyan,
and the great flood to the west, the new America;
the endless weeping at doors and harbours,
enough to make starvation seem a luxury;
I remember Europa and the white turbine.

Think about what they want to escape,
to face danger and at best indifference;
show me Kurdistan on a map,
show me the remittance economies of faith;
he is not my brother, she is not my sister,
from darkness to darkness I lift them up.

*

I am Leukothia, opening my arms to you,
the wave rises, turning limbs in vaulted light,
I hold you in my hands one moment
magnified before the white crash.

Pytheas

I am Pytheas of Massalia,
I sit and watch and drink.

When I speak I am not believed,
I will die on this dockside in the sun.

I watch the ships sail away and return,
captive in thought circumscribed by Strabo.

                *

I sailed into a greater knowledge,
driven by a curiosity stronger than any trade wind;
I saw all the things and places I tell you.
I did not follow a picture of the world,
whether from Miletus or Egypt: I looked,
I saw the invisible Isle of the Pritanni.

I talked and bartered my way across Armorica
to the sea at the supposed edge of the world;
the trade in knowledge was local,
what Agde knew of Carcasso and Carcasso of Gironde;
I joined each link with my own hands,
then took ship from Ushant to the tin islands.

I cast my words like rope to secure the boat,
pulled into harbours for which you had no names;
we stuffed our boxes with gold and silver coins,
perfume, coloured glass and exotic trinkets.
We were hungry for tin, the magical alloy,
to run the arms race against Carthage.

Has the world changed much at all? I doubt it.
Are there still elites and prestige goods?
Consider who wants you not to find out for yourself,
add it up, exchange outside theogeny;
for immediate and dangerous knowledge
I swapped gifts with strangers and stepped ashore.

The great ocean put the chill in my bones,
I stood on the promontory called Belerion
bright and shining one, after 95 nautical miles;
this single fact dismantles your geography.
I crossed the land bridge to their market,
saw the Pretanni work the tin in clever ways.

The painted ones called it Albion,
Apollo flies at the back of their sun;
island by island and further inland by foot,
the flight paths, alignments, circles of stone,
rectangular fields and riches buried for gods;
after 95 nautical miles I measured it.

*

I wait in this room over the drink shop,
Winter wraps a cloak around the harbour.

Water flops against the empty quay
and light in waves spreads across my ceiling.

My dry bones whisper the great ocean,
open the box, a knucklebone of tin.

The Ingliss Touriste Patient

What do you mean too late? Is he in danger?

And I was afraid and thought I would die,
lifting off the table, only the ceiling above me
and the vertiginous air for your voice Melanie.
– Yesterday you should bring him, you must
be like sleep now, you must go to the hospital.

Next to Yorta, unconscious – ella Yorta, ella ella,
wake up wake up my daughter, my child;
Yorta – Aorta – Iota not caring one jot,
there's something wrong with a letter,
a letter is unconscious, a letter is Maria's daughter
next to Aorta, mine, something is wrong with the invisible.

Stand up.
Close your eyes.
Stand feet together.
You have the hurt problem.

I was there and not there,
under the great weight of the water
with the silver jackals and companions of the sea
suspended by a taste for the shape they once had;
diamonds of light dance over them,
they sit in a shining circle and grin,
– look at me, look at these anchors, look at these roots,
– down here the mind is overcome.

And I was there and not there,
wheeled off to brain scan land.
Where is my wife? Will I come back here? Where is she please?
Πού είναι γυναίκα μου; θα 'ελδω εδώ πάλι; Πού είναι παραχαλώ;
She's with the gypsies from the big camp
sliding along the corridors, riding hips,
I was back in the cardboard town by the airport,
– where do they come from?
– from here, they come from here.
Sliding along the dark corridors,
her hand holding up the baby's head to light the world.

Gracious Maria found us cold water;
she sat by her daughter all night,
drowsy Yorta recovering, Yorta the beautiful,
and Melanie thanked her for her help,
– oh but we are all people, yes.

I was there and not there:
Pound in the olive grove raging,
a ghost white man waving a broken branch
in the perfect climate for the human nervous system;
the olive tree blown green and white and
the air like a lens for the Earth given a fair chance;
Pound went down to the ship, Europa, the wreckage,
raging, raging at the innocent ants of my harbour,
its arms open to the various world.

I was there and not there with my wife and my mother;
we stared at a small television at our feet, the size of a dark
                                                    footlight;
it was the emergency services concert,
– firemen, bare-chested, singing Bohemian Rhapsody,

which was not to my taste;
we stood around the dark hole at our feet,
companionable and variously entertained.

My head was away and singing:
an' war'ly cares an' war'ly men/May a' gae tapsalteerie, O
my girls wait by the sea, longing for the waves,
green grow the rashes, O standing up so straight.

My head was away and singing:
all night I saw with my eyes closed
squares of blue black landscape,
villages and tracks, cisterns, temples, bus lanes and hospitals;
a series of design features made for civilisation
before it was named; and talking and watercourses,
a mythology rising at every turn, local, particular and useful.
At last with my eyes open on the first day,
surprised not to see the landscapes imprinted on the world,
looking again and again, I was ready.

From Cambos, the air heavy with eucalyptus rolled over the car,
sweet pine and burnt dust off Taygetos drenched the road
and through Kardhamyli jasmine in waves fell upon us;
so you kept driving and I lay down and the full moon
made its path across the water and I was there.

Helen Mania

1

Helen didn't want the trouble
safe behind those walls
the army of the fertile plain said so.

I looked at Marathonisi, plotted
the chariot tracks crashing down
from Thalami to Pephnos and the sea.

Helen didn't want it to happen,
then love like Paris arrived.

I looked at the serene harbour
isle of fennel, empty blue mirror,
Helen was not there nor in Egypt.

Honey melting the other side of Taygetos that night.

2

I set my foot in the track
greased slot to smashed Ilium,
one way ride to bliss or exile.

Night of stars, night of revelation
silver jackal sniffing around the door
storm came smoking off Taygetos.

The house became a boat and
the great green flooded her mind
the island, her dream, floated out to Paris.

Snakes and figs littered the yard.

That morning Helen threw aside the carpet of stars
that morning Helen stepped aboard.

3

We fled in the hour of the furnace
Helen a black outline in the blast
dark one, I see only your face.

Swing the pendulum myth
another woman, another man sail eastward
pass Cythera, ploughing the grain.

Aphrodite came swanning out
attendant gods swim in their wake
their mouths shaping O O in the eddies.

Oh Helen I loved every woman
to have you, Mr Meat me, the fool
to find you deep in darkness.

4

We saw the sun burn the high meadows
the rain drench the white roots
the wind fuck the come hither waves.

We ran up the goat tracks, breathless
between spurge and aconite and mallow.

Helen you have undone the world
I taste your looks, touch your colour
you were always there, my radiant lexicon.

See how our boat dips and rises
to our shared step aboard
noses out of Pephnos over the endless sea.

We lie together in the seabed
just rippling the light with our breath.

from

Your Thinking Tracts or Nations

(2001)

In 1996 A.H. gave K.C.
14 pictures for his 40th birthday.

Between 1997 and 2001 K.C.
wrote poems for each of the pictures.

Picture Three

Here I am and what a postcard
from the green capital of the singing world.
What is it that we do in music,
made visible in the trees above our lives?

When I arrived in London town
the monuments danced in a round;
the theatre places were closed for plague,
the far side of the river hung with shame.

To make it new I opened my big mouth,
in green fields of Lambeth, by water meadows temple,
I made Master William hammer a ladder out of song
and ride the leaping horse of day up in the sky.

When I sang river song, my head afloat,
stones moved and the banks collapsed;
radiant classicism went straight to hell:
but still, a sound, my name, fills this other air.

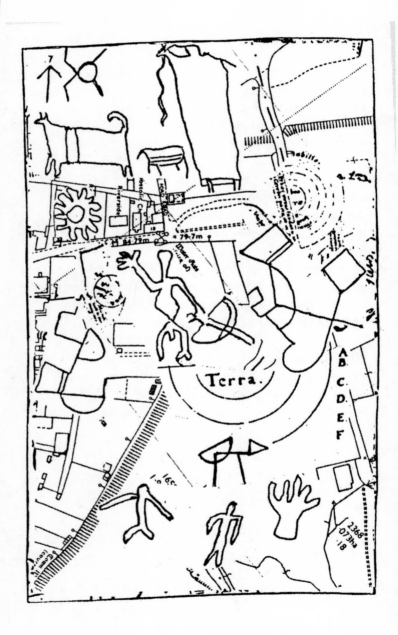

Terra.

Picture Six

'At the same time the mind is trying to find its place within
the land, to discover a way to dispel its own sense of
estrangement.'

(secret letter to strawman
home secateur dear Jack)

Give me my death back
I will free me if you do,
what I saw killed me right off,
give it back to me yours.

At the core endless white
terror at the other pole terror
the mouthless singer, the shadow hunter
at the same time the mind.

I could not move my arms and legs,
they were too far away;
I could not make a word in my mouth
I was suspended in a shaft in the earth.

Then I came to in the forest
of hands, the sun red off centre
over the dark utilitarian units,
the private calibration shot.

You must walk on as if I were
an open door, go right through me
as you go, you will feel nothing
in the great whiteness roaring.

Jack what I saw killed me right off,
Jack give it back to me yours.

*

I shot across the frozen lake near Ratzeburg,
like in the poem, Sarah, splintering at speed
a road straight through hell, a road,
ice breaking like thunder islands of ice

absorbing the mind's self consciousness
in attention to the object working on it;
I was a rock in the Arctic ocean dreaming,
ha, I was a painted rock upon etc yours

later, I don't recall, a hand reaching out,
you were not there, a pitch of nightmare
a motion of its own, I swam in solid air
as if falling cadence after cadence

at night the sky full of stars, the moon rising,
after three days the first ice appeared
—growlers, boulders in a river, in deep swell, hunting us,
then we dropped below the convergence

Laudanum gave me repose,
a green continent of fountains
trees nodding in the very heart of waste,
the fields, the air, the sun, made new

one word undid me: riverside, to sit by a river
in England—riverside, with others, to watch
the river flow under trees in green shade—
undid me here in this unfixed place.

*

(Amundsen to Cpt Scott)
Beg leave to inform you proceeding Antarctica.

*

The home secateur has asked me to write to you in response
to your letter on extreme metaphorical climates. You are
mistaken in blaming the home secateur for such conditions.
Whilst it is the policy of the government to listen to the
concerns of the public, there is currently no policy on the
matter you raise. Indeed if there were such a policy no
government official would be personally responsible in the
manner you seem to suggest. Moreover the home secateur's
experience of such dilemmas is bound by EU conventions,
the correct observance of which, makes his personal
responsibility like that of any private citizen, yourself for
example.

*

I could draw a map of the place
from memory, the striped animals,
the handsome food running about,
the small bay open like a mouth for trade.

What if I let the bloody history in?
Imagine: when they came with the goods,
a tribe iron-shod, iron-bound.
How come they have the goods?

I think in the centre of their minds
danced an armed man, a-jig, a-jig,
in that alpha beta of six sounds;
I - Want - You - Give - It - Or.

They left no marks in the snow
but the host of the air in our blood,
then all my own relations
gone like the drifting smoke.

*

We wore animal heads
in the fat time of plenty.

I don't know, shadow of a bird,
let me run, they are good shapes running.

And it was a garden to us.

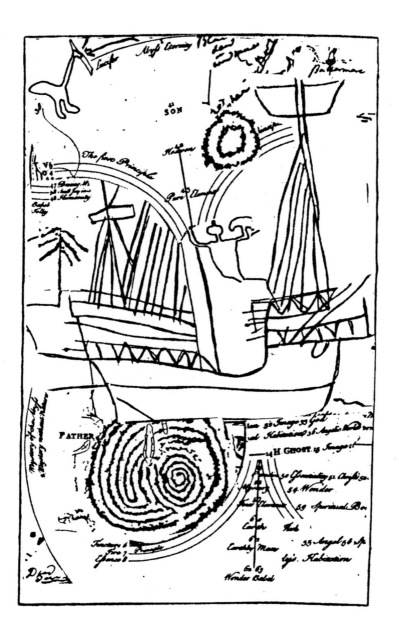

Picture Eight

When the great drift set in
I suffered the isolating vision,
eyes down the dark tunnel
blind to the white zero of spring.

We had to pass Sikinos
then return on the empty ferry,
Elytis walks the rocky terraces
myth hard as bone.

In the wake of thought,
in the deep bays of the western approaches,
tell me the names the catalogue of ships
Eng-a-lish literature in the offing.

the Bolivar, Don Juan, the Speedwell, Ariel,
the Chepstow ferry Sam, burning like beacons.

*

Their ship made land south of here,
soft underfoot the rancid classicism,
not so much vision made plain
but sex changed to politics.

You see that spirit hovering there,
she tastes like honey, dark in dark water;
she backs everything we say—we make it up
the vine, the olive, the mimosa singing.

As if Europe did not mean to set foot here
a great turmoil drags our thought,
then a sea so still every rope was reflected
and boards cracked like shot in the heat.

She is over us and under us;
the vine, the olive, the mimosa singing.

*

On the island, heads full of the sea,
what we took to be metaphor was fact;
to write each name and cross it out
did not change a thing, we were there and it was real.

In the holy period of Spring
the moon rises so fast it tears your heart out,
it does not ask anything
making a white path on the water.

In the square the local children sing
a bloody minded tune,
modal, Ottoman, clawing at the dome,
the mountains ascend like music.

Let the lost villages rise up in the sky,
mapping out an empire of light.

*

Only one boat will take me from here,
a black boat, animal head at the prow;
she stands by the tree in the bow
she stares low across the water.

Alan I am out of the picture,
if Coleridge had gone with Leake
we'd have the place mapped;
I am standing on the edge of the world.

I am reduced to pure white bones.
I am compact, immutable, absent.
I was drowned in a jar of honey
but my brother, the snake, gave me back my green life.

At the edge of the world is the great sea;
only one boat will take me from here.

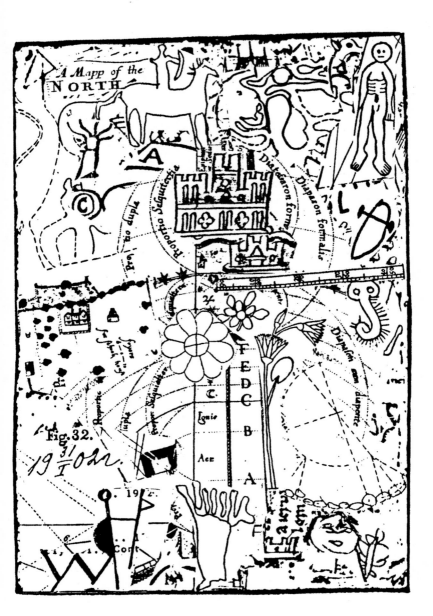

Picture Eleven

I remember at night the glow
of free running food on shore
and the simple boy staring.
O yellow flower, ace of ambition,
our cathedral and powerhouse
the charge folded over in time.
If I peel back that cloth
crawling with beetles and polaroids,
there's no mystery there I think.
Across the ditch and ramparts
we see the dreaming blue distance,
the secret lakes teeming
let in our veins each spring.
Fat heroes on horses came,
hoards from the north in quotations,
they shoot at you, sharpen the pointy arrow
as strophe in the new order.
O yellow flower, ace of ambition,
I remember at night your glow.

*

In the frozen fields of the world
poets die   of frostbite or anger
like any other body.

Call him Shackleton, our captain
I back every word he says,
his signal runs to the ends of the earth.

The dead sail out from Possession Bay
hang suspended below the line,
black ships on shadows rise and fall.

They don't dream of pasturage,
good horses and green invasion,
of the alphabet ascending.

*

Accurate estimation is difficult,
the clear air, the monotony of colour,
in our minds the Paulet Island route.

No more books from him,
a glacial period scrapes off the faces of home,
of children, the pretty words moraine.

*

We lived in the old house then
held by deep fields rolling down to the river,
like silver snaking through the hills;
hunter-gatherers would glide by on yachts,
bargain for souvenirs, hunger for fluorescence;
when they left we called it a movement in history,
when they returned we called it the weekend.

We lived in the old house then and everyone
who danced and made music for the god
wore masks, we got up on our toes in season;
we did not think it was popularising
nor pushing back into darker fields:

let the rubble tell you, put your face in that mask;
my eyes sharpen when big night comes.

We lived in the old house then, backed by mountains,
you think we've gone, into the dry river bed, the hills;
but you imagine the beads and not the thread
as if we left a series of pictures but no words;
then, when you rise along the dusty tract,
on the next step up you see the blue surrounding sea
and your mind is flooded with us.

*

Across fields silvery with democracy
MacSweeney's borage blooms
and poets die of frostbite, anger, bad luck.

Black wing spread over them,
frozen sky folded over them
a picture of the world turned upside down.

The light in their faces ignites,
each pearl snapped off the endless thread;
what life is left (is left) in words(?) ?

What happened to those slow evenings?
the easy music?   cold breath
of ice caves took them.

Across fields silvery with democracy
where MacSweeney's borage blooms.

My Life With Byron

(2000)

And Such Other Cudgelled and Heterodox People

Climbing the liquid stairs of drink
we go   are you there Alan
in the English good night
where Byron glides unwritten.

*

Across empty England tilting under cloud
towards a new order and petrol thirst,
trees lift like visions at the margins of fields;
an innocent history passing with ease
as if the rural poor lined the road, waving.

Blasted through a slot together landscape,
with no essential link between these lives
– easy as speed, didn't feel a thing –
dead winding gear, wooded fields, barracks towns,
figures moving together in a film.

To answer the young lord's questions:
we can commit a whole country to its prisons,
depopulate and lay waste all around us and
restore Sherwood forest as an asylum for outlaws;
in the English good night, where Byron glides unwritten.

*

In the cold eye of the lake
light dissolves around the trees,
a boy, free as a fish, dives
dreaming of the sea.

*

Lyres on earth cast like nets
to catch the living god
but to stand beneath these walls
and fall into those hands is terror.

The beginning is music, a strange thing;
in the shade of power we found ruin and delight,
crossing Paynim shores, Earth's central line,
through an invisible door.

Over the dark sliding wave
into half the world unknown,
with liquid nerves in charged air
we sought the god of birds.

Saw the blue cape afar
said his heart, tamed to its cage
all summer long;
milord is dreaming an island of light.

*

"I ran to the end of the wooden pier... the dear fellow
pulled off his cap and wav'd it.. God bless him for a gallant
spirit and a kind one."

*

After an interval of years, this composition to one far and firm;
events left me for imaginary objects, an imaginary England.
Do you remember when we were out with the Luddites,
from airy hail about the county, about the forest and villages?

But buzz buzz eager nations, not with human thought,
no new land nor fair republic, no deep sea music sounding.
Events left me in the umbrage of green shade,
my dear Hobhouse, return to that country.

In that completed state words are things,
the electric chain we darkly bind about ourselves.
From this tower of days I see the pathless woods
and the waters washing empires away.

*

excuse the scrawl, fresh morning at daybreak
boat starting for Kalamo . . blue upon blue these mountains,
the Turkish fleet gone, the blockade removed

the air fresh but not sharp, we sailed together,
the song we sang was – a nation to be made,
when the waves divided us we made signals
firing pistols and carbines, tomorrow we meet at Missolonghi

if at the head of some one hundred boys
of the belt and of the blade, that I may
(calculate the cost of keeping one man in the field for one month
                the sale of the Rochdale manor?)
we bore up again for the same port

excuse the scrawl ..
frosty morning that means to be of promise,
that I may get the Greeks to keep the field

the final port or [word torn out with seal]
who will stick with the Greeks now?
the Lemprière dictionary quotation Gentlemen

or those who do not dissemble faults or virtues?
(when I was in the habit)
I reserved such things for verse

*

Aboard the Florida in an oblong packing case lined with tin,
organs and intestines in earthenware jars
– *this heart should be unmoved* –

The case stamped with seals of the provisional government,
painted black and submerged in a barrel of spirits
– *worm, canker, grief* –

Hobhouse went aboard at London Dock Buoy,
the undertakers were draining the barrel
– *life blood strike home* –

Though assured "it had all the freshness and firmness of life",
he declined this last view of his friend
but later identified him by his foot.

And John Clare, wandering down Oxford Street,
saw the funeral train and a girl sighed – *poor LB* –.

*

To answer the young lord's questions

Saturday night at the trough
they talk about technology,
new magic make you work harder,
their veins corrupted to mud.

I can hardly make the words out,
I never saw such things in the provinces of Turkey;
men sacrificed for cheap exports,
for Spider-work to bloat others.

The magistrates assembled,
troops ransacked homes around Newstead;
men, guilty of poverty, wanting to dig
but another owns the spade.

This mob enabled you to defy the world;
the poor pitched against the poor
must learn flexible work and slut-time,
must learn global economy.

Capital tips off the edge of the world
to strike the old deal still in place,
a life above ground or boundless waste;
here we go, here we go, here we go.

Breakers of frames, iconoclasts incandescent,
let me be among you about the county;
snap their heads awake
with the politics of paradise.

The Ludicrous Placation of Ghosts

Beyond my hand and the round eye of light,
Byron, Jane Harrison and my mother
stand in the mist of Niagara Falls.

They stare at the wall of water falling,
decked out in the tourists black poncho,
the water falling a thousand feet.

In the great rush she looks at me
with such courtesy for the living,
then steps into the beaded air for ever.

*

His shoes were black and shiny,
he danced across the Irish Sea in 1946.

Spic and span drill in the holy orphanage and British Army;
I'm not making up a word of this.

How wide's the Irish Sea?
How deep the coastal shelf?

*

They will not eat blonde food,
think of Dumuzi, his snake hands
                his final descent,
–dig a trench to the west of the tomb–

They will break a contract of shadows,
they long for morning air, on the street,
to walk and let them live in us,
—look along it to the west,
pour down water as purification, then myrrh—

Some sounds some burdens can release,
—do not name the dead—
some sounds some burdens can release,
—but they will have blood—

They know there's nothing like the world,
they cannot make up one word of it.

Catalogue of Ships

Aboard the Princess Elizabeth, the Lisbon packet
for the Vathek theme park.

Aboard the frigate Hyperion,
big sun bright sea the land of.

Aboard the Townshend packet,
Captain Bucket at your service.

Aboard the Spider for Prevesa,
Missolonghi over the water, low in the mouth.

Aboard the Pylades, quick step to Smyrna.
Aboard the Salsette, salt it for the Hellespont.

Aboard the Hydra, transport ship
stuffed with Elgin's plunder.

Aboard the Volage, sweet frigate.
Aboard the schooner Bolivar, oh my Bolivar.

Aboard the Hercules for Cephalonia,
an unnamed mystico, an unnamed bombard, fit for song.

Aboard the Florida, down the blackhole
all the way to Hucknall Torkard

Where Cain stands in a spotlight
and nothing flows from liquid space.

I walk with dust in peopled darkness – come.

Ambelakia

All afternoon the birds of Ambelakia sing
and the air is the shape of itself
rising in one breath to Olympus and Ossa;
that light should have substance and sound.

The Common Company of Ambelakia founded 1778,
founded on madder, sheep blood and method,
the red dyed cotton of the first co-operative.
"We have decided to renew our company,
spreading a table for all . . in the dress of communication . ."

Schools Libraries Hospitals Mansions Welfare

In 1811 Ali Pasha, sociopath and maverick,
admirer of Byron's ears, raided the village.
By 1820, with the rise of Manchester as king,
the fall of the Bank of Vienna and the war of greater powers,
the beneficent society collapsed.

Remember the Common Company of Ambelakia,
the first industrial co-operative.
Remember schools; libraries; hospitals; mansions; welfare.

*

The painted ceilings and walls of the houses
depicted real and imagined cities,
young girls gazed down from balconies
and the world abounded with birds and flowers,
as the high meadows with aconite, anemone and cyclamen.

The full moon is high tonight,
the spring sky milky with stars;
other villages cast like sparks
shine out across the valleys.

The Objects Were Not Paid For
Or Got For A Fixed Price (Elgin)

As they lowered the last metope marble rain fell on their faces,
"Telos." The Disdar stepped into history and with him the five
girls crying for their sister, the ravished one, ready for shipment
in the lower town, filling the air with lamentations.

The events dictate a mythology of fact and we wait for the girl
to return in Spring. "Milor explored in the bowels of the earth to
dig them up." Milor stole gods to that coast of no return, to the
shadow world below this light; the triumph of Eng-a-lish classicism.

Milor ripped the Panathenaic frieze from the walls of the cella
where the goddess dwelt. It is the procession of all her people
translated into stone and she the city incarnate. "To realise its
meaning we must always think it back into its place."

Of the money Elgin received half repaid to the government in debt;
the objects thus an integral part of the British Museum collection.

Sources:
1st stanza, line 2 Clarke; line 4 Douglas.
2nd stanza, line 3 Benizelos, line 4 Byron.
3rd stanza, line 4, Harrison.
4th stanza, line 2, Chris Smith.

The ivy on the wall lifts in one wave
as summer flares into the sky,
a pattern of streets, a map of pleasure
rising deep in the green cell.

If it pours in over our eyes and mouths
light flooding through limbs,
the young green hands
hold us breathing under water.

Then a door opens deep in the cell,
you hear the music of all your life:
to go in is dangerous,
to turn away is dangerous.

Brother to the snake, in winter riot born,
let me bear your tattoo;
light splashing from leaf to leaf,
glossy cups scandent for the god.

They knew what hit them
out on the coast

        sky black with ash
        earthquake
        tidal wave
        fire

They knew
a crowd on harbour street
white stones bordered by blue
a crowd in one wave
sacrifice   to get at the life again

If this is a poem
about the death of
the one the many
there must have been children sleeping
in sweet abandonment
as the unknown sailed into the harbour
and the world stopped

Even the air of the high peaks
thick with ash   bitter mouth
even the blood dead   they knew

Late at night another station fades in,
late late, when only security lights burn;
this is news, another station,
Orpheus ascending in ritual intervals.

From the archives of Radio Sofia
a language I don't have,
Yanka Rupinka, Kalinka Vulcheva
– sung on returning from the fields.

Nerve stripping voice, unearthly scale,
my whole life pouring back to me
at ground zero, I hear it fade out in
a table song by different means.

Early morning frost this morning,
white ghost packing blue fields away,
turning from night, these counties
run to the capital, pale horse racing.

Thinking your dark body asleep in my hands,
thinking big sun raging
from a slab of marble sea,
anaesthetised by Duveen out of Elgin.

But to wake on Ossa in spring,
at each step a grove, a secret stream,
the air rings under an endless sky
waiting for a figure to appear.

In delight a door opens in the air,
we see the whole of Thessaly rising.

Disclaimer: ~~Byron Never Went To Ambelakia~~

"I saw before me in the vivid occupation of the people of that
place a living notion of the world made good, a species of
heresy, a society unfallen – just suppose this were known in
England – the very thing I had traversed the theatre of war to
find, here ..."

He saw the Common Company of Ambelakia working,
the houses, the schools, the three hundred workshops,
he saw Shelley plain and the technology of genius.

As polyphonic bird song filled the air
he saw Ali Pasha's troops rise out of the Vale of Tempi,
indifferent men climbing the foothills of Ossa.

To exact murder, taxes, arbitrary arrest,
invisible powers of empire on their backs,
he saw the same beset the Nottingham weavers.

He saw the enormous condescension of posterity
rise up and he retreated into the house of George Mavros,
all thought and poise gone.

Milord knocked clean off his box.

from

When Suzy Was

(1999)

Hotel Byron

From Hotel Byron the wind slips over red tiled roofs
bearing us back into port, one more day.
The red and black banners of the KKE
stretched tight as sails above each street,
— they think Lenin lives still in Moscow,
    nobody tells them, so they think it still.

Above the sea, a village of old people,
— You Italiani? America? No, Anglos.
No bakery here, at night the dark sea speaks;
no pirates, no Turks, no baker.

Our faces sunk in Saronic blue,
we suffered confusion, the last car fading.
Small boats scud and arc across the bay of light
and you make those shapes with your mouth that I love.

*

Laconic

Kranai   Marathonisi   isle of fennel
one fisherman   the still waters of Githyon
the sun rising

Kranai, Helen said, so
tell me now and I won't ask again
and with morning they sailed into myth.

*

The choir of many voices sing
my heart is broken, oh
the bird flies from the clearing.

How one sound, all my life I've heard
our mouths close around many shapes
possessed by death, by vengeance song.

Deepest octosyllabic land
oh my heart is, the sea rages
make me see what's in front of my face.

                                        *

In the fast channel of Despotikon
I married the sea, the gold circle sank
to surface in a dream all night.
Out of corrugated light; give it back.

Its white absence aches on my finger,
stolen from sense to the sea bed.
If I could work it out
I would know you again.

There is:
the apparent surface of the water;
the light in the body of the water;
the unknown ground under the water.

It sank because it was an object.
It cannot be lost, love has no weight.
It sank into irretrievable regret.
Give it back.

*

By Monday, at the end of the world,
falling in the dizzy air of Cape Matepan,
the lighthouse, the cornflowers alight like blue sparks,
no birds calling the last step down
drowns us into the submarine cave called hell.
You can get into hell. It's not literature.

Each separate light a white path on the sliding waves.

At the end of the world, ships pass bound for Crete,
blue devices low in the water following a strange trade.
We lost track of days and the meaning of number,
heads empty to the waves speaking the first language of sense;
island to island white spume ripples the shore,
a whole country rising up in free association.

The Book of Answers

We sat at the truth table in the quiet house and I told Lee
about The Book of Answers, as a way to try to think about
what is always there: the alphabet, an etched model of silence
that speaks. (Nonnus) My conceit to make the physical
condition of language, the arrangement of the struts, curves
and sounds, the form of discovered truth. Completely simple
questions. To think about what is always there: reification as a
type of behaviour in the moment of the poem.

We took the short walk to the sea,
turn left from Lee's house and it's there;
a silvery band across the end of the street
the sea charge sparkling in the air
in the bright almost early Spring day.

Lee pinned his answers to its open door:
to measure the medication between pain and clear thought;
to listen to the radio;
to do more each day;
to read Lynette Roberts;
and by April to be out and about across the hills.

In the Red Book

I'd like to write one poem but darkness is down,
just one word — the water's running against me;
fingers tied in knots and eyes gone
filled heavily to the shape you see,
but one spark, lie down you stupid bugger, lie down.

*

We kept to coastal routes, in sight of meaning
around the shores of the various world.
Held in a disc of swimming light, miles away,
a picture of the park; under spreading oak
the exiles relax at last, their children playing.

I remember in the red book a diagram,
trade patterns put food in our mouths;
those people from across the great green
at that level of sophistication inventing surplus:
you are dedicated to trade and you to magic.

Carving this seal in carnelian, a fingertip across,
dolphin accompanying other fish, will ruin my sight
— and you to magic, just different work
in a disc of swimming light.
Look. All the trees gone for ships.

Ash   Elm   Boxwood   Maple
       the pollen levels sing from a pit
Olive   Vine   and   Fig
       the land is rising to meet you
In the red book I am a small axe.

*

The fleet sailed from Stonypath;
the Temple, Precipice, Sphink and Fortune,
away for the Gulf boys, on the morning away:
scattering salt on the white world
all bright and sparkling in its wake.

The Literal Poem About My Father

There's nothing like music,
certainly nothing like the music in Enniscorthy,
cracked and sobbing republican songs
sung in the face of the Black and Tans.

Those murdering bastards from Glasgow slums,
for what they did to the priests,
nothing like the tuneless drone from upstairs
and a curse on the morning for what they did.

Each night we breathed a drunk's mythology,
the English officer and sweet colleen;
the drone's in the air around me still
though he's in the ground nine months now.

When my mother was dying I was strong,
I hit first and faced him down
all my years boyed up against him,
but for all that it's like he never was.

An alcoholic given to violence;
a thief; an abuser of his children;
an arsonist who was finally sectioned:
each term I secure for clarity.

Where's that Johnny Corcoran,
the little Irish man with all the kids?
He is gone, gone, gone,
four daughters and a son angry with a dead man.
Gone, gone, gone.

*

Again I think I drive the old road
but it's the open landscape design
and the memory is stronger and physical.
This is where the old road was,
the look of the trees, the nearby village
— it's not there, the place is changed,
and the people at the end of it gone.

Out there, field upon field of darkness
I don't want to be out in
but on the narrow rise of the old road;
descending into the next town
the pool of light of streets and houses
I think I drive towards,
each time along the flattened route.

*

I thought I saw my father
walking towards me on the street,
though he's dead ten months now.

It was another man in the crowd
but he looked as I remember him:
short, compact and fixed;
a trouble to my mother and sisters.

I catch my breath before the truth,
watch him go and fall in the dust.

*

Lee I was thinking of what you said
driving to the next town
through September rain and landscaped roads,
there's no end of things,
the good is the fact you're writing.

I think the trees in the wet fields
lean the way of the coming truth,
to return by instruments, by earthly stars
mapping out a restored country
as darkness falls in each fold.

My children talk themselves into dreams,
our hands deep in the sea of glass,
we rush to the edge of the known world
where the road ends in air.

When Suzy Was

If I look up from here
glancing off the picture David sent
I can see Skorpios across the water,
owned by Onassis, empty and unvisited.

At night navigation buoys burn
five fixed points in a line,
the island is a picture of death,
a dark thought in broad daylight.

Hermes, psychopompos, took the man down,
rising beyond the private island
the Pindus mountains make no comment,
drowned in miraculous light.

*

For the dead I love to dance in their bodies again
the house is too small in fact,
the decor rustic haute bourgeoisie
— death turns a delicate ankle
it looks like his veins need stripping:
"We could do a deal ..." I think not,
climb over the counter, forget the books.

The trick of separating them from their lives
gets underway before I arrive,
numberless they clamour at the window:
this one thinks if only he could arrange the letters

it would make all the difference; it won't,
the matrix of dots but motes in the air.
When Suzy was a skeleton she went rattle rattle rattle.

What strikes me is how flat it all looks,
despite four grown men going mental
pressing their faces into the room,
and they become four deaths: mine.
The books bake in an oven
in a frenzy of vowels sans sense;
don't pretend you hear distant music.

*

It's futile to confuse my girls' fatal serial song,
the empty island of a dead plutocrat
and the printing house dance;
mountains and islands rising from the sea.

In the village an old woman stares into Madeleine's eyes,
she wants to hold the young girl's face,
it is a marvel to her, she shapes the air between us;
they're face to face and the air is still.

When Suzy was a nothing, a nothing ...

In fact the dead have names;
my mother, my father,
Stuart, who died aged 22,
my two brothers who died as babies.

They buzz like nobody's business,
they flicker against the tiny panes
— let us in, let us in;
invisible everywhere in the picture.

She used to go like this this this

God Is Not a Ventriloquist

I'd thought to make this book a version of the oracular process, to find out what is always there in the making of the poem; ambiguity, bounding like Koretas's goats across the high meadows of language in the Spring of the god's returning.

Imagine the inquiry as the unearthing of the poem. The descent into the adyton, coughing up fumes to the Pythia's raving; revelation for others to make sense of afterwards. As Pausanias says, "... when she descends into the place of the prophecy, she does not take with her any kind of skill or talent." So, I thought myself well-qualified.

Holding a cord to the omphalos, and in the other hand laurel, she is possessed by the young god. The god's words are incoherent; at what point, and by whom, the meaning was fixed is unclear. The priest as exegete delivers the answer to the inquirer. I see the ritual, in all its versions, as a blueprint for introspection at the centre of the world — the thought of it. Three impersonal figures hold as functions of the making mind: inquirer, possessed and exegete as one.

Though I'd thought to make this book
I don't know ... in the place of calling up
let the wheeling sky come down,
wash these hands and cleanse all fault.
I am the brother of the snake,
I spit laurel between my teeth.

The Name Apollo

Apollo, god of words, accept my song,
let it rise like an arrow
the voice and flight of birds
[unblown and pure into the sky]

strike out into nothing,
into the [empty] air of spring
and satyrs enter, in revel, saying whatever:
I know another returns, I know

by the ivy tattooed on my arm
[the silver foil] the pigeon feather,
the flight and voice of . . . .

You don't wrap it in mystery, in proscription
Apollo . . . . I do the work of vision . . .

*

I came down from the northern forests;
furs, wax, honey and slaves:
they took me to their coastal cities,
merchants, craftsmen of the wonderful art,
from the inland sea to the ocean.

They took me for their own
to those islands I was borne;
her arms around a single tree
in a soft meadow split asunder
in the centre, miracle of light.

In my bones the white north sleeps,
each winter I return there:
they are children in the garden
making magic with stones
and hidden designs in my name.

*

I was the chosen boy, both parents alive,
no touch of death, in the place named for me
a boy leading boys.

Dressed in laurel, dressed in light
the waking dream of spring
parades from door to door.

I took the year from the earth,
the flight and voice of vision,
made a hole in the ground speak.

The Roadside Shrine

1

As if by arrangement four figures are spaced evenly in the foreground of the photograph; a road sign, an old man seated on a bench, an empty bench and a shrine. The road runs around the southern slopes of Parnassos. The view drops into the deep river valley, make one mistake and you die. Beyond, the mountain wall of silence rises out of the frame as you stand with your back to Delphi.

The road sign is a red circle with a red diagonal through an old fashioned car horn, more like a bugle, meaning prohibited - don't touch it. The silhouette of the old man is at rest. Hat back, walking stick propped, he looks into the valley but not, the angle of his head suggests, at the sanctuary of Athena below.

Next to the empty bench, the roadside shrine is a blue display case on stilts, topped with an open fretwork cupola and cross. With glass on four sides and the mechanism on top, it could be a crane operated lucky dip machine — the tension in the claw set so that nothing of substance can be lifted. The air-blue wooden sides are weathered, the door oil stained.

You stand with your back to the sanctuary. The road is empty on a morning in Spring. Scattered with scrub and gorse, the white mountain rises.

2

The candid mountain shines
through the blue fretwork dome,
the shrine glides over the valley
a broken television on the air.

Tangled scrub surrounds the case
visible through glass on every side,
blown and spiky, a promise of life
against the dead contents exhibited.

Inside, a cameo of the patriarch
stares above a box of matches;
in the centre, a framed Christ,
casts a picture within the picture.

It looks as if sea and sky
meet in line with his shoulders,
an ouzo glass of oil on water
stands in front of him.

To the side a plastic coke bottle
ready to refuel the flame;
in all this sky and mountain
interior darkness absorbs the light.

3

In this case all we have is the succession
of deities and the memory of uncreated light,
the faded grey blue of the central figure
— a young unbearded Robert Powell cum Byzantine androgyny,
the panama halo and gaze of utter blankness
in the face of the sun as great iconoclast.

To open a window in the sky, the copy must be perfect,
as in, "When you see your brother or sister, you see God."
or, "The best icon of God is the human person."
We should praise iconodules, in particular St. John Damascene;
"... for the flower of painting makes me look,
charms my eyes as does a flowering meadow..."

The Coke bottle, fixed in plastic, does not shine,
a corruption of Samuelson's 1916 classic;
the figure dull and thickened out,
"aggressively female" as Loewy said, it sells plenty,
but in the wrong way here;
the label script full-frontal and invisible.

In the ouzo glass, viscous sunlight glows amber,
appears to ignite the oil without burning the wick;
light catches on the right of the frame
lending definition to its cheap detail:
neither effect is proof of anything
but the great Spring day rising on Parnassos.

Catalogue of Answers

a white-painted bull
on a floral background

*

mistress of the animals
tree goddess . . .
snake goddess [with] us
sea goddess
one with . . .
[mother] goddess
lover
she is kourotrophos
she carries the young god
in her arms, Zeus
         boy of boys.

*

In the bright vision there are magical animals
and indistinct human figures. That man is armed.
Below us fish swim a crowded sea and to the right,
away from the page, Asia is a model of the world
around its red function.

Look: the birdman steps into the green field site.
All about him the blatant geometry of planning
cuts in; an axe throws light on the issue. If any
straight bearing is finally a powerline we should
leave now. The tectonic plates grind against each
other at the committee stage. We should leave.

*

Oh Oh I am north, a frozen mapp. Shrunk to
the core in my tiny house, under a sky of
ice-floes, tinkling.
Let the yellow flower rise, let it radiate
something. Feed me you sub-atomic, half-life zoomorph.
From the door of St. Magnus the men of Orkney
went mad for Egypt, roaring an alphabet of
hot triangles across the great green.

*

On these short days the roads are frozen solid,
no-one moves in a nation seen as traffic plan;
at the ice station we imagine the flight path grid,
the god of frost grinning.

Incoming control, packed like cold affronts,
government by insult out of spite:
from every house a line of music soars,
thin hope scales the glass sky.

To unsay one thing fit to sing, most probably,
turning each sheet of ice,
scratching black words to sing or else
give it up for the lusty sparrows.

Full of fight, sure of breath and mighty,
a scatter in the frigid tree.
Sing up, sing up, you querulous sods;
burn the branch to make spring come.

*

Woke around three this morning
to the yelp of foxes mating
somewhere between the backyard and Chinese restaurant,
ululating in strict measure, under moonlight.
Retake the republic of feeling,
such cities and temples beyond the art of Phidias
and from the anarchy of dreaming sleep,
retake the republic of feeling.

*

I found her in Myrtos
sleeping by the Libyan Sea
by lemon groves and burning rock,
with sixteen different words for blue.

My village goddess;
her elongated head and neck,
her accentuated breasts,
her blank and dreaming face.

Worn and naked in my hands
all of eight inches tall,
she carries a water jug
out of red earth.

*

she can dim the morning light
she makes me talk
she gives me my life
she can fuck me anytime she likes

*

I know I pursue the impossible archaeology
of the restored family album,
most of it sold for drink
– wedding photographs for the frames,
their bed, the radio, her clothes:
our belonging particles somewhere.
What we can tell of their lives is by what's left.
The old man sleeping on the floor,
on the eiderdown with two pillows
exactly where the bed would have been.
From a great height we stare down
into the pit of generation: look,
the framed cast of a man asleep.

*

they thought they saw
in the meadow by the sea
a white bull dancing

*

That morning sweet birds
made small pools of sound,
one music   a message
from the waking god.

Kastalios said, where we go
they are like us and unlike us,
we will barter with them
and keep safe in coastal waters.

What we see as islands
are the peaks of a lost landscape
the seaways open at first light,
who can read this waveform model?

We did nothing to make it happen,
the big dolphin hit the deck;
first fear, then radiance
– after that the ship was not ours.

Kastalios spoke out,
we followed the bounding youth
as if dancing, inland,
we forgot our homes, our wives.

*

The field of understanding, Pound said,
and how to extend it, imperial measure:
tin from Spain, copper from Cyprus
with gold from Egypt as payment,
to run the arms race against Hittites.

The field of understanding, but not
an equation as yet resolved,
as metallurgists did not say to the great Wanax
when, one bright and focused morning,
subsistence became surplus to feed experts.

*

static singing the arc of days
losing all trace, I touch
the alphabet of knowing shapes,
the dark substance of a music to make you free

as if the coast of a continent
rises into view on an undreamt day

ascending on a child's breath
the noisy birds, Siobhan said
they're so noisy, they want to speak
people language like us

*

another night, tunnelling
only nocturnal systems for sound,
drunks, traffic, domestic machines,
dropping a rope into the cave

dreaming of external light
the marble quarry, a white field,
a promontory over the sea,
figures waiting in the ground to rise

stone axe, obsidian, emery
enough to shape gods

*

from

Melanie's Book

(1996)

Wait for the light under a canopy of leaves,
casual music burning the crisis,
time to get literal, the man said to the man
message comes out all the same.

Estate by estate, family by family
the poor turned invisible,
the hard blue sky above the stadium
currencies vanish, nations appear.

Saturation coverage tells you nothing
I was thinking in the water, on my knees,
the new year rolling across the park,
you already know it's poetry.

Men walk like this, women walk like that.
Our sense of purpose would stun the traffic.

The family radio was smaller than the fat battery attached to it. We kept it in a tin; twanging Duane Eddy, the Shadows and assassinations echoed out of a metallic past. Its casing was sky blue with a silver plastic grid over the small speaker. The transparent, circular tuner had a serrated edge for a better grip. A blood red line picked out Athens, Moscow, Luxembourg, Athlone.

O city city. Turning. Turning.

*

Over a doorway in the museum hangs the salutation to Parnassos, 1904. At the prow the leader raises a chalice. A dozen red, fleshy men eyeing each others' muscles, row towards the distant mountain. You see this from the bow facing the toiling pairs, caught in Biblical exertion as the choppy waves break on rocks. Truth spills out of the picture, the chain that is round us now.

My arsonist neighbour lights another fire
dirtying the end of summer, Moscow burns,
smoke thickens – ignore the words, listen to the tone.
Can you cope with this one in a golfing suit?

The room fills with smoke and all sense evacuates
– if I stood up straight the line would be unimpeded –
and longer than all the seasons rising above the white desk,
he lost the inward walk, promenading frames at an exhibition.

Variously orchestrated the moon rests on the hill;
the air is softer than a hidden message,
the airwaves carrying Russian music, American poetry.
We'll conspire to forget the world, whatever it says.

There are moments of Biblical rhetoric here
above the loaded tray, telephone, assumed narrative;
I would rather talk to you in the light,
not rub anger into it at 2 o'clock, 3 o'clock.

We float away from England, mapping the brittle voices;
our house at night is full of noise, ringed by fire
– if this is what happens I feel cheated –
and nocturnal animals pull at the rubbish for love.

If I stood up straight the line would be unimpeded.

Earth at night is an uneven smear of lights;
America, Europe, parts of Asia, the Gulf,
fires burning in rural tracts cash the crop.
It's homely, a light left on in the dark;
earth at night is the pattern of money,
a squid fleet off Japan, gas flares at sea.

Below red cliffs in the narrow channel
the days pile up in line astern,
stupid in the mouth of the good time.
The trade route takes you anywhere;
along the streets of a new nation
imagine the film of all these faces.

In our lives country music's literal,
sounding out the low place of compromise
the money sets in all our hands;
we turn into the darker wave,
we touch the ground and keep the deal:
a river of silk pours over the desert.

In the middle of the journey,
the straight way lost,
we came to a dark wood.

Pine needles for bed,
branches spread across a sky without depth,
you felt the earth swallow you whole.

Your cry startled a bird
Your breathing the beat of wings,
April sun ascending.

We came to a dark wood.

There I'm thinking with my hands
and the room's flying over the city,
over the bridge, the parks and zippy motorway
your open face floating before me.

Everytime I see you
something happens and I can't speak,
like birds in the air
calling and calling your name out.

That will do in plain speech
against what we don't know,
the burning traffic takes us
wrecked on the far side.

There aerial words wait,
unequal to your next breath.

In the dark car staring
the whole sky unfolds before us,
over the fields and silent roads where we must go,
your face and the stars
and the great John James line,
'...here in this your poem and mine. I beg you to free this boy.'

Whilst other activities tap the window
we move inside each other,
your perfect body calling and calling glides over me
tier upon tier I rise in cathedral light,
my mouth opening inside you,
in all this darkness only your taste,

Here in this your underworld and mine
I beg you to keep this boy.

Night rushes in at the car window
lighted houses and cold miles westward,
later, in the hotel we hear home drift away
and an owl calling over the border
over the dark hills and rivers,
there your face is changing above me;
love pours into us and we cross the threshold
writing a page from Melanie's book
– nobody has loved me the way you do.

*

Inanna Queen of Heaven and Earth
everything flows from you, you go to hell for your lover.
You're the Queen of Heaven and Earth, I thought you'd
                                        want to know.
– You know how to stop a girl eating her breakfast don't you.

*

Out into the white morning
we were surprised to see other people alive
going about their normal business,
for we know this world is uninhabited.

The river rose in the night
flooding the winter fields,
a slow thought emerges,
frozen by morning.

All this landscape stuff?
Just ice age mud and trees,
I suppose I live here now,
unpeopled more or less.

At night we burn,
I look into your face
and the world's made dark
in the music of your red mouth.

Thy faire vertues move me,
not to use one word for another,
perfect sexual beauty
say my name over and over.

One night we walked across town under the blown stars, with all the damage at our backs it does not come well arranged. Dark houses piled up; try lust, pride and covetousness. Try closing the door on that lot, domestic gardens alive with those animals.

We saw the fox eyeing cars, staring into the moment of impact then sauntering off the road, to leave a fox-shaped hole in the air, for all the traffic in the world to drive through.

Dark houses piled up. Close the door. The fox stepping in and out of life in front of us.

In the dream I was driving down a narrow lane to an English village where I was born, or through a dangerous and disputed border country.

The lane narrowed with overhanging trees and the hedgerows pressed in. I was lost and stuck with no way of returning. She beckoned me the way through. The colossus of earlier poems, dead now for nine years. All proportion is thrown.

She kindly takes the car and drives me through the tunnel of trees, the car is hers now. Her worn hand rests on me and I shrink. She reaches through the windscreen, which dissolves, and removes obstacles from our path.

She stands looking at me as I leave the car, I'm in exactly the right place to set out across the open hills. Then I know love is not a metaphor. Her love surrounds me. It has only one name as I leave, turning to tell you when you wake.

Cruising away from England at 33,000 feet
we saw you and waved but you didn't look up,
playing in a bright green square
your faces rise fresh in my mind

In the dream of falling I wanted to jump,
rush into the circuit of states and sculptured coasts
the real map of the air of desire,
dense like the language we spoke

Saying yes you would, so we jumped
bouncing off the wing into the blue harbour,
watching ourselves fall onto Cyprus
into the poppies of the necropolis outside Paphos

Oh set your arms around me,
hold on and let the wave lift us to the shore.

By the harbour an off-shore island,
out of the air above the waves
Theseus abandoned Ariadne,
previously geometric, previously unknown,
you take a step down into the sanctuary.

Eating the fig in the shade of the well
we were drunk with seeing.
One time you could smell what the boats brought in
slice a tomato and smell it
like that, on the other side of the street.

Beyond the causeway, out of the sun,
the swimmer can see the submerged town;
collapsed doorways, shining paths,
step through marbled light, on the blue threshold
into deeper pressure I heard: Hello boy.

The sea rolled over our heads,
the thought of the next island or another person
ended here; the body of water crashing about us
delivered one word – love
and a terrible fight it was too.

Athens

I saw an abstract concept of human form
outside in the rain of Monday
turning cold with autumn.

I saw you across the room
your good legs under the table,
the sky opening our senses
everyday this absolute music plays.

In the blue field carved from the block
without loss of reason your life appears,
you can get personal about it or not.

Hands reach out and lights map
dark streets and familiar traffic,
in this unimagined town I imagine
I see your eyes, your face, your colour.

Athlone

This afternoon a summer wind
revealed the underside of leaves,
fields in waves all the way home
made green light to swim through.

I was the boy again, it was my picture,
look at these colours,
it was summer rolling out
and the personal dead lying down.

There are things not said in poetry:
the personal dead and the lying down light,
this casual breeze all over England
and the boy I was afraid to meet gone.

Nothing is lost in all that time,
it's my daughter saying – look my picture.

Hilversum

Saxon mouth, telling us how to live,
over the scabby allotments back there
but for the warmth in the name
even my sister, what do you expect?

It leaps up from the long table into your face:
at 1.20 dread wind slips into town,
at 1.20 total loss holds me.
There's no stepping back from here.

Standing outside the house
I thought we were dark bodies
walking through the light of facing windows;
another family lives there now.

It means don't believe that broadcast,
the time of your life or.

Home Service

Driving away from there
ground fog ankle deep in meadows
live radio cast before us,
the car packed with trophies.

Westward into big sky
deep in the dark fold,
ghosts drift over the fields
each boundary lined with snow.

Night silence gone down the tunnel
our view is immediate landscape,
the wealth of supermarkets
exploding for sheer enterprise.

The external narration is nothing.
Stop. Unload. I know where this can go.

from

Lyric Lyric

(1993)

I run to some farr countrye
where noe man shall me know,
inside, working at the walls,
my hands misread the truth.

Western light falls away,
houses write against the sky
economic miracle as fact,
scaling the big adventure.

Bright logographic news
wraps around the shape of days
a gratuitous statement of class,
pressed home from out there.

Make a list of all your worries:
human and animal signs,
parts of the body, speech,
— grammar the lot.

It's you you you, a man's voice
grr   oon   gri   hh
hits the window like grit
filling the dark house.

The moon frozen in blue suede,
framed in a loom of cables,
left me standing alone
tilting traffic off centre.

Air filters my window,
my face, my table and literal sky,
a door into the river night
the site of deep assent.

I could write through the table, cursively gouge down to the hieroglyphs living in our capitals. B, E and M are some of my favourites; house, man and water. Dusted with logic and sand I set them right against gentlemen thieves burning in the east. The dirt piles up at my back, tradition blocking the stairs and the light at the bottom of the stairwell.
— Are you alright down there Linda? Is the baby alright?
Is that smell December outside the window damp and rotting into latent spring?

The tunnel down is steady, the trees overhead let fall unfixed statements. If I have run carefully, watching my tread along the dark stream, then all things will settle into all things and I should arrive at absolute normal breathing the air of a new speech. Look at the sea, its immense rolling indifference, I love it.

It shapes the words into packed cars, children, medieval stripped pine garden tools, tight jeans and living spaces. It's entirely sincere and doesn't feel like a fetish. There's a substance to my neighbours that you can't see through. It doesn't look like economics. Are they agents? Are you? Circle each precious name.
— Everything inside is mine, it took me years ... All that stolen time, never to be returned. Then whoosh, the centre dysfunctions, an accident or failed organ. Everything gone. Look at the sea.

In the turquoise mines
at Serabit el-Khadem
our lady of turquoise
letters the first alphabet,
ten years to read one word.

Lady of turquoise
in the river country
freshen our mouths,
around this garden
we know everything.

Blackbird sings days end
glazed light rays spring,
money burns the path
sex turned inside out
delight lay before us.

How can we ever, that carpet,
I shall pin the dumb song moment
familiar shapes inscribe
man, woman, driving home
return me word by word.

'Looking for the source of the chill in my bones'
Jack Spicer

I took advice, travelled north
and jumped into the ocean off Cape Wrath,
ocean is an expected word I think,
a vast body of water sloshing about;
endless, deep and cold,
giant stacks aloft spinning the unfixed sky.

I had a conversation there,
piano music and no sleep,
a vast body – nothing said nothing;
I listened and spoke, tidal washed
submarine rubbish, like here, discarded:
imperishable plastic, gulls and jaded wrecks.

If there was a figure in command
he was not there, he had no shape,
as water is in water we walk through,
against the laws of erosion
a slow current sang,
    If I was the King of Ireland
    and held love that was not power,
but destroys all the same;
I see you falling
across the sea bed
a band of light, insane.

Tocharian the I-E Enclave

They say there is, along the silk route,
a life away, another language like ours,
used by people unlike us

Its way is lined with hoardings
across the figure mountains, real mountains
that will kill you if you stay out too long

A few lights come on in the darkness,
yellow squares draw in the day
it is the absolutely normal

We watch the cars, shop for leather shoes,
check the post and think of a reply,
begin a working day eating English breakfast

It's only a sustained analogy
I've never been there of course,
I'm right here telling you

We live east of the Altai mountains
oasis cities in the steppeland,
we light our streets, pipe music all night

Imagine the postmark, the stamps,
our busy trade in visions,
outside is only arid and nomads

If you speak like us say so

The garden surrounds me blowing
these disconnected, separate powers
through the air space. Who owns it?
Glitzy helicopters come and go
in the Spring drift above the town,
the centre traffic free, barricaded;
tubular sections of concrete sewer pipes
await the arrival of the prime minister,
all day, all day, this grating noise
shreds the sky in filmy strips.

Washed up on non-specific virus
lethargy spreads like summer,
I see the small child crouch
eye to eye with a red tulip,
in a moment of stillness
stick her fingers in the cup;
the flies and bees start up again
weaving the square of green and trees.
The world is all that is the case.
The world is the shrine.

There's a lot I want to say in this voice,
tilt my face up to the sun
and work from the centre of what is.
Say some Chaucer to us, the young girls said,
imagine that music begins afresh;
outside April rain through sunlight
shines the fields and beaming hills;
say some Chaucer to us,
and all the other traffic vanished
whan that Aprill with his shoures soote.

I read in the dust one morning
— He is helping to distribute the crops —

I work all day to earn the money
to buy you things. I work all day. Fullstop.
You know that tune, I bought my love a fridge,
now there's nothing we won't do, all the stops eroded;
three hundred yards away, over a barrier and flower beds,
a jerky grey midget walks her goons,
dressed up power gone in the mouth.
Shame on you. Shame on you. Shame on you.

Music Of the Altai Mountains

Comes to us from a distance,
it's not ours but an air surrounds us
in broken, ambiguous clouds,
a voice sings four sounds simultaneously
longing for the real to start up
in classic loose cut denim;
the hills are alive, you're not fooling anyone.

The song continued a day and night,
face-up, clearing out the house,
absorbing shapes of rain and shine
the stars and remote traffic,
transcribing the garden fathers' talk,
a fox at the rubbish, a car door slam.

All you see is drawn into that closure,
there's no technique there,
no interior, instrumental light for bearings;
you think you're trading with the enemy,
the inhabitants armed to the teeth
with the culture they despise,
look straight at you and ask one question.

I think it's your eyes that do it,
alive like the sky flaking away
forms such as never were in nature,
these words made for your mouth
name and strip the margin
between here and the blue folder.

We go up town for clothes,
working over the white table
in purposeful music and movement,
sends these loaded terms, your steady look
out of the window into Spring take off,
the west everywhere reeling.

It looms behind plate glass
wrapped and cushioned in lace,
rank and pink, the perfumed heart.
What can you do with it?
In this heat   on the bespattered pavement.
What?   I was walking   and you

walk by the river in darkness
where the water flows with ease

John, that passionate man, in his action tower
held like a thought over London mapped
lights living patches to the hidden river,
an underwater bass singing its heart out,
the books are safe away, in his generous hands
a thousand anonymous musicians go dumb
waiting for one book only to appear
in this floating room behind the glass.

I woke up on the two lane section, roving
westward into rain county literary guide,
the cheek of it unfolding, a thing to say,
I woke imagining each station struck one note
passing at speed heard in sequence,
all at once, a static song laid out to home
intone little pressure changes in the ear,
drop down, leaning forward open mouthed.

What am I doing here flying over England?
at a nasty tilt, green fields and conservative clubs
flatten out like a grid to the Irish Sea,
off the road are houses where children live
and the heads of the republics return to the centre,
the country looks like a picture of itself,
state the name for it, petty towns and news shows,
drawn in the wake of a commercial van.

Tony and Liz

John Dowland in the passing traffic
goes over my head, parched all summer
those names fly, all summer long
in a hot room, in a hot town, I freeze.

Shining Tor   White Peak   Manifold Track
the water table, the truth table, logic gates
diesel wind diversions on the motorway,
oh you noticed all those old songs.

This could be a driving poem but for
the invasive smell of shit in Staffordshire
and Tom on the tape saying
'colourless nation / sucking on grief'

Here we are in a music house.
Shining Tor   White Peak   Manifold Track.

in the end you could find an index
my eyes on springs season of love,
season of gaps in the grey air,
just flick through the green pages
the ghosts say what you don't say
those people locked up without cause
their hands are empty, their mouths are empty,
against ironic commentary
the poem a hymn to the republic,
my name and all that history I suppose,
a dream book called correspondence
was whatever was happening and who
driven from the capital
under a sky of stupid messages,
sound tunnels lined with hoardings
the ruined traffic spirals
I would make go the other way

from

The Next Wave

(1990)

pale hole winter sun
punched in the sky
draining the year
frost solid three days

ultrasound interior
dark heart beats
as though unfixed
in monochromatic inversion

blind, buried alive
already kicking
we saw a head, spine
stomach, limbs and organs

night driving darkness
I think we saw
the leaping god articulate
and day rise to sight

Deep waves form in mid-ocean,
the stuff is in my mouth,
riding the tube scattered farmers
bear the living work
arranged in Asia Minor,
trouble makers and migrants
toil all day, read all night,
transparent speech and trade
reclaim the perfect body.

The idea was simple;
banish feeling to the borders,
fallen sky flapping, back lit,
civic contact bitten down to sense
tariffs and national traits seal it,
heretics singing all night duty.
She said to her companion
– it's too stupid for words,
what happened to the forward man
pressing through crowds,
just one poem would do - no chance.

Ride up hill after work,
fields brimming left and right
sing one phrase over and over
the moon's face above,
a tree sprayed fountain
beads shivering arcs of day,
vapour trails X dark sky
nothing good on the breeze
but wood, wet leaves, smoke.

One thread of light levels the west,
fire burning the new homes;
bow down presentive hosts
over uncertain ground
mud, cowpats and grass;
there's a pure music
driven in the details of our lives
rising like a signature
action and bright meanings tend
that look in your face,
time goes down before it
holding there the vigil.

Inside Britannia

surrounded by the words I reach
'the sweet hollow by the broad bay'
tar, peat, dispersal in my mouth,
I thought in serial, number, doubt

the system's ruin was its strength
a corpse touted in the streets,
no I think the tongue
spoke advantage in strict measure

hard work of all those years
made ordinary, knotting hands and back
twisted into fact
dumb mimetic exile lore

walk into the thought
moved on the floor of the house
catwalk figures dictate
a modest proposal brought home

then, without panic, finally myth
turning on the air
the silver walls go down,
I want it now I want it

there was no body, no crime;
go home to nothing 'spirit',
we should like letters
to correct the infraction

the captive children bounce
in castle pneumatic,
mums and dads drink
gothic Disney country song

hands across the water
around the throat
construct another career,
the tower of power poem

true sailing is dead
the lesser for the greater,
if I was the king of Ireland
level the fake colophon

dark patch burning
bunched like a fist
in my sight flowering green
my palm, this page

in that human age
polyphonic work song
developed to such perfection
work ceased for its singing

below the retail pavilion
trope a public square
the light of truth sinks,
casual but smart, true but false

her features tender stone
taught me hard facts,
engraved? nothing in it
how I miss you are there still

taking objects for words
tasted and shaped in the mouth,
the Great Hall of the poem
rose above our infant might

I live above the shop. I see things. I hold that tone as darkness comes from the lighted window. Your ref. none/amount £22.50. These people are rich because others are poor. I think the sky is a cage without music. Inside a character says – Take your hand off my gun you little fool – and the barrel gleams metallic blue along the street resting in the parallel track. The other voice wants to do a deal – I am a man with a torch in my hand – and the scene lives in the flame. A lady from Eng-a-land sent money for the burial of the animal. The colours blend, sample and lie as the days fall out untouched. The cold sun shines on brown and grey roofs. I saw a picture like that once. It was called the invention of writing.

They limit public thought,
–really? Yes, it's a sort of picture language,
–what do you do? I drink, I sing,
thinking how I wrote that poem;
clouds drift over the hills,
a man at work in the grey
points a red flame, memory drills the roof
leaking light and money.

I hold the baby in my arms,
your life, the line drawn across it
and medicine for sore throats,
these clotted buds of speech;
our lives attendant and detailed
sleepwalk the amnesia pretone.

from

TCL

(1989)

crowd driven in the deficit
much like the back scene of a play
or melodrame
                think of something else
that life
seeking my father in the dust
magnet in hand writing
that life over my head
consumes itself but one
the Co-op manager singing
Zion beautiful Zion
all around the estate
and it looks like
– I don't know what

The Strange Visitor

Soon after a stranger called on him. From inside a voluminous coat, folded back like idle wings in the night, the stranger drew out glistening sheets of gold, malachite, lapis lazuli and realgar. With a whiff of the stage magician more used to entertaining the infants of bank managers and pornographers the stranger set the colours in a waterfall, making a cave of his room; each twist revealing visions of small places, street maps and lives running on in the fold and flutter of their semaphore. A suspicion of trickery, combined with a knowledge of English poetry, formed in his mind. The visitor made him understand a story.

> A man came to feel that he did not fit well in his body; his hands from the outside were not his from the inside, leave alone the organs and appendages. The condition expressed itself in crime. Some of the crimes were invisible but others meant unmanageable pain to someone he loved. He dreamt himself into different times and trailed text book symptoms of anxiety wherever he went.
>
> At night the dictionary would spontaneously combust and his past vanish. After damping down and reconstruction the frazzled lexicon would assume a nasty utilitarian aspect, usually with a beige interior that promoted murder by squalid husbands in at-home-clothes. They hung about in doorways and bemoaned the strictures of subjective political action.
>
> Their block typified the neighbourhood and was the fortress of a civic hell. A steel ladder was fixed to the tower and sanctified by aspiring politicians who flooded the residents as they climbed; dislodging the innocent and guilty from their sofas on a tide of commodities and shares. In the swill the intricacies of the certificates were redrawn to read yes and no simultaneously.
>
> The ill-fitting man wanted to know what had happened to him, what had happened to his people.

The colours had stopped and he was waiting for the story to end. He shook and drew back the curtains. The gloom of another nineteenth century dawn advanced and a persistent novelist lodged narrowly in his mind began to shave the former experience.

Work Song

three nights cranking the rack
4.30, 5.10, 5 something obsessive
cold stars the winter
drawn across both ways

bent low over a rocking table
fix one word to one word
for joy against possession
to turn the beast and thrive

step into silent darkness
thinking a tower in prose,
radio Jerusalem short-wave
cradles the earth boustrephedon

'Let me get on top of you
Let me make you happy.'

Not The Sole Relation Of Human Beings

Back bent fire hums,
immediate work against glitter in hands,
at the dumping end of bad systems
cars drive off the plot
all young couples have
in their first freshness
cut like breathing stone.

Through luxury afternoons,
looming gap and moral choice,
the account came to ape itself;
blue townscape cubes scatter
stretched sky unravelling its edges,
we enter the religious theme park
riding waves of logic, regret and spite.

Then the Carlyle quotation –
it means more than money,
she reads only and ruins lives – quietus –
around the tower of blood
they shall be enskied,
children dodge sniper fire
what you say limits the place.

Rubber cathedrals and indifferent adultery
anchor the crafted shires,
anything but thought;
over the wall April sweeps the street
someone planted those daffodils
they come so fast, smell of rain
air waves house lights all night.

Shakespeare clouds bank abstraction,
bloodied merchants hold the stage
Roger Scruton the foyer,
a varnished face sipping wine.
What are you thinking Roger?
Balmy white man rhetoric
nailing the victim to the crime,
bound for the terminal hospital
hands and heart made private;
your mouth breathes manifesto
gilding the Belmont gloss.
Let me be, this May night,
straight as an arrow
the regenerative status of fact.

Watching the honeysuckle pour
clematis starred over the trellis
sun stares birds swoop and sing,
talk of the devil scares the populace
encircles the world set aside
tactical problem and grievous error;
shooting the newly literate,
the malnourished, the darker than yourself.

What place can poetry make?
Who lives there, so mirrored?
Empty inside the glitterball
dim, cosy, unmoving continent
below this peach honeysuckle
clematis starred spilling out in May
I read a few days off;
slick starlings sharp as bullets
hit my neighbour's table, eat his bread,
shit on his sheet and fly away
– here's a good bit, peck peck;
strictly speaking they don't talk
despite the flight to speech as prime,
the future falls from the sky
white blobs drill a Midland or Northern town,
outstared in the silver stone
attendant lords range rove
cower, smile, laugh full-throat
catching the angles, teeth.
How's it going? ten seconds
the one eyed camera states,
eight seconds popular dissent,
pull away – shoppers, dancing youths,
script cut dog-lick.

Working from the blueprint
fat bees drift in the garden
grass greens between us
rain wet path lights the sun
strong as the aversion to death;
the dream an endless promise
narrates first names with all accretions:
commerce, nature, the pit
fresh cleaned, a pebble for the shot.
No creaking throne comes down
the boys to please break the book,
a hoot and a holler away from paradise
broad air burns filtered days
travelling light caught in the net
calloused finger tips probe:
clouds, shoots, the personal life
distended plans run wild
– you don't feel but do more.

Megaphones clot the streets
police drive in the eyes,
I mean sentences,
stars fixed across the screen
a sort of machinery is at work,
dumb song compulsory
enthralled by vacant ghosts;
buried back there a dead body,
candid, coiled and waiting
– they fear it's a woman
with shoes to buy,
biscuits and mince in the bag.
Let me stamp it on your head
feel want, taste grief, need friends,
lie down, forget, don dark glasses.

Sitting in the bank I hear
music from out there, a girl's voice
flung at a reckless pitch in early summer,
monitors flicker ups and downs
in the house of the rising sun
locals share fossil fuel signs,
her daddy was a gambler,
you can ask for further details
you are in the hands of callisthenic management;
pavement softens to a hidden depth
waving trees line the road
shaping a V into the sky
it goes out at a certain point
chorus cracks ends in step.

Cleaning out household rubbish,
durables that didn't endure,
that state which is one, indivisible,
ceaselessly changing, already gone
I'm in two minds about it;
drilled with summer rain
orange groves wrapped in filmy heat,
the plain coasting down to the sea
as different moments in the same thought
beat across the ceded ground,
memory cast to landfill sites
remains something else
no matter what may fill the gap
– the man from Del Monte, he say starve.

You can't always pull things in
from outside the sun is bright,
it is spelt SUN in a circle,
I read about the origin of the lyric
saw the face of the teeming world
but communal work songs, who knows?
The national grid nets the brimming air,
all thought gone story time,
unloads lives in clipped terms
X fact the ever after poems
thins cloud to frame a scene
a bloody trench of English boys
dead with nothing to say,
an obliging vacuum slams the lid.

Under the shadow of how it happened,
ur-heimat in the racist mountains,
the Magnetic I sails forth
to name the bigger light
seeking advantageous terms
and a subject to predicate;
all references to money are analogical
as in, I can go on or clear out
ideas that have no currency
arresting the big adventure,
a worn coin burns your hand,
dead soldiers, scientists, poets
stack their faces in piles
the corruption absolute, normal.

from

Qiryat Sepher

(1988)

I dreamt my house a film,
Frank O'Hara got clubbed to the sand
sweet, tough and dead
his upturned hand lay in the surf

ideograms pinned on the dock wall
read – the day will change your shape
you are not the same as morning
sliding across the uncial sea

open my eyes, sweet birds sing
I take these chains from my heart
St. Gregory composes a world
an ivory book cover carved in light

we three scribes work in the crypt
balance the floating crown and palace
bent and empty heads
see it all with blank eyes

it's hard work, you bet
the poor boy had one book at home
Treasure Island buried in the attic
neither was the sentence in his grasp

every sand becomes a gem
in the fiery circuit of the word
knowledge is power
you can not blot it out

Nobody thinks hard enough for poetry

I've walked through their town
but nobody thinks hard enough,
the distractions are many: novels, news,
people and moving pictures in boxes
– you've never seen the like
now the rain hits the window
on the hills it's snow, an English spring

actor poets prat about in arts labs
they rage and imagine a vain thing
but their art is a contrived sloth,
I think they don't concentrate
not on one single word,
one book dropped in the letter box
would burn their paper homes

marooned up stage mouthing air
mighty history glares down
that's our history, the cyclorama
where everything is at it happens
buried and shining in the streets
the articulate speech you taught me
my kind king, I send you a line

Qiryat Sepher

at the end of days in
the city of the letter
traffic blocks the streets

shoppers look convinced
but only next to money
signs and values abound

unearth the native script
to free the falling crowd
– it's £19.99 I think

Adorno

there are powers make the girls dress up
moist at its root and barely hidden
markets speak the jargon of authenticity,
boys with haircuts like their dads

a girl in gothic style freewheels
the fountain of gods and tortured horses;
Neptune topped with a parking cone
salutes his prick-like head in praise

what do they really say, what's in their words?
cars glide by and we're in it deep;
sassy pavements melt libidinous summer,
terminal shop of slashed prices but no jobs

the poor families sweat a golden aura
drawn through their skin into nothing

I get sick of this common secrecy,
make a silver cube of days suspended
rain birds singing, rills and gists

my fingers inscribe initials of white vine
children marching home in unforced actions,
only the bullets are plastic before the fall

but shooting the rioters is the riot;
Bee four God we will pull down all the mills
we will amend the terms of our containment

Not the chocolate box pictures but the village and I
shouting down a green tube of trees and rapid growth,
he saw a common treasury in this compound body
dancing upside down in the palace of famous murderers;
the content changes just like us
following that line of force all week
the ghost ship written out of the log
floats into the poem, with an arm here, a leg there,
an act uncontained by that book or this;
the box featured politicians with new teeth
ready to do the great things we once did, rejoice,
eat lunch as the frozen waters of the world ignite;
under the lid bread and circus sweets poison the kids
the whole lot topped off with feisty tits

That's how it works, one century overlaps onto the next
like a fold in the domestic mountains;
new by-laws were displayed in each town and station
behind mesh wire in blotchy, black capitals,
everyone knew the unfamiliar terms at once,
the sanctions read like odes reaching back
their first homes made of care and soft stone
each family restored before the European night,
one word, one place and well known sites;
the tailor's hand ran smooth and quick over the hills,
a journeyman carting his politics about, each day
the tidal wave brimming behind the next copse
shakes the pretty leaves, breathe on me breath of
– I think they knew it was other men up to something

from

The Red and Yellow Book

(1986)

she smashed the glass and swept it up,
at home a husband of 56 year old baby fat
followed me through my life
Spring rips through the world, everything looks good
this is the fifth line, made it o.k.

– it was a petrol glass

you breathe out, I hear cooking
imagine rich people with emotional problems
it's heaven, it's probably Paul Newman
and certain domestic appliances hummed on,
I think he can deal with it

paintings in hospitals can help;
local scenes, the haywain, a good frame
or the two cartoonish kids looking at the moon,
they are folksy and sit on a bench
they are rumpled and happy

– I am not joking

You should know voices when you hear them;
sparrows, dogs, post vans and neighbours
lilting and damn the pastoral
but the dark all around me
held her head up
and shrank to nothing in a white bed

the last poem

– no death is an average death

I wish I could get my voice back oh

the fields where you grew are burning

– would you like your bed jacket now ?
Yes   I   think   I   will

fear no more the heat of

the last word –drink–

8.50 p.m. 9 August 1984.

– we're with you mum (kiss)

in my arms, all gone
a mannerist portrait
58 years old, all gone

I was with my mother when she died, by the bed in the corner of the ward. Quiet after visiting time; her brother and sister and my sisters.

The doctor had said at mid-day, 'It won't be long now, she'll soon be free of it.' I went up town to buy the ginger beer she wanted; small bottles with screw tops. My final thing for you, and until this last day you held the glass yourself. In the teeth of death a human act.

The day before I'd been called back to the hospital to get rid of my father, drunk and talking about euthanasia. Only the medically qualified understand alcoholics. He left noisily, but she was beyond embarrassment then.

I sat on one side holding her hand, her sister on the other. Through six months she was gentle and kind to us all. I could feel no strength in her hot and cold hands.

Her shallow breathing stopped, stopped, in suddenly, taking the chin and lower face as well; not her face then. I watched the last pulse in her neck, kissed her forehead and said, 'We're with you mum.' Then the sister said, 'She's gone, she's at peace now.'

I was with my mother when – after so long it seemed hurried

a gentle woman of great strength
she raised five children in love

snow falling in pop songs dumb dumb
what do I do tomorrow whilst little shapes
falling skid a rubber car down canals
with horrible echoes all over the rock
two lines of traffic, brake, can not hold that shape
how do tomorrow when others jigsaw talk,
his teeth in your mouth
snow falling on the whole world, crepuscular and infected
the light wheel flutters in my hands,
this is it – with no control you carry on
If that's the case I'm leaving

double pearl, fire and ruby bear her name
how did it start snow falling ?
mountainous sky of non-verbal weather
experienced antibiotics in nervous tracks
across the sky opens snow and out falls
a complete town; powder of light, the many lives

Why don't you lift the piano lid to play that tune ?
it's not a piano, it's a poor metaphor;
see my fingers presentive,
presentive fingers playing a metaphor
like polar bears dive from glaciers to fish
or my foot arch curls with secret warmth;
the final continent beyond analogy
here are the poor, they have number,
the adults with worn hands of too much care.

the sky hits your head, it's so cold
a door slams in your chest
shock settles like breath in the garden,
chestnut leaves falling on the grave of Martin Heidegger,

that wave held be careful how you drive
foam engineering, a lorry takes a corner
a string of red lights comes on
against   the   iron   hills,   age
ancient Europe, those people up there
that face looking out for me

from the Red and Yellow Book

the house fronts flip over
subterranean rivers surface in
public fountains of gods and tortured horses,
brown and rabid near the rapist's car park
the grand sweep of the municipal offices –
see the hand moving, its trick
the truth has made us free

*

clouds pile up in the sky
anvil   lemon   cicatrix
with the industrial revolution
marriage, divorce and public health,
William – it was English poetry too
in the circle of our blood
blinking like moles through the other side of winter,
in the fields of Peterloo
in the valley thick with corn
the kind man reads a world revealed:
honey flows in the sky
piles of soap and hot bread
in the streets smell the earth,
bright buds green as bullets
the polished cars and public lies,
they are what they do

*

to find the western path
I breakfasted swords big sun
                    gates of and
at first breath   bird song
happy in the stupid heart,
the fool with his finger on the trigger
no further forward for men and women,
hot days of rubbish letters
surface to surface arrows
telekinesis and country music
spark across the imperial world

*

rain on April streets and cars
the occupation forces hold the populists' gazebo,
no sweet moderation shines in Port Albion.
walls of sound of sea has made them soft and witless;
hamsters in perspex balls
daffodils and socket sets
markets crash and banks roar,
they dream wealth creation in elected bodies
and we all fall down

*

another life in a sparrow's wing
spreads above the prisoners,
running through the desert
they leave coils of rope and clouds of red dust,
having modified their experience
the look of the sentence and the title
emanated a spell – shazam –

the bristling globe, the shores of men and women
silk descending folds around
the piano keys nervous itch
as Jackson Pollock trees scratch the sky
balloons absorb each other, the green garages
and unknown pedestrians in an opera of no pain

*

just look, In-der-Welt-sein
but nowhere to park the car,
it rains local newspaper lies
about a town nobody lives in,
it means a fistful of mush or
darkness in the kitchen on tottering legs:
in seed time learn the beautiful history,
I must wash my hair
I must be happy
                    the first
dictionary had only four words
I will tell you what they are
You will live a better life

*

open your hands, let them go
there's no going back to that world,
this room has many pictures
I think of that beginning book
silver tried in a furnace of earth
up to the elbows shines in words
before meanings, the restraint is all
as Spring rattles its couplings,

birds fornicate in bare trees
the light flicks a switch in their eyes,
fuses blowing everywhere
the dark earth and its smell
grows onyx, carnelian, quartz
the fifth and greatest monarchy:
I know you in my hands
the level streets of a life before us

*

day into day, night into night speaks,
far off and exceeding deep
in all the houses that are lived in
broad sunlight through the air,
I buy a pineapple at the Chinese grocers,
warm that house, it's Greek to you,
a woman is wearing pink trousers
she walks in morning and legs
open shop doors, the happy actors on their blocks
write sky on a banner above the street,
they pretend everything is O.K.
a street in the sky, the real sky,
in blue capitals, the language of delivery

from

Robin Hood in the Dark Ages

(1985)

Deeds

the many facets of it, the radio
like bowls of light of thickening
walls what they say neighbours
in orbit about the heart a human
world as obvious as phenomenology as
the mind becomes actual here in
the European winter I have lit
the fire we have a mineral history to burn
and we can't keep our hands off each other

your face that night through the windscreen
warming up, no satisfactory explanation I
have my wife my friend it is a Brandenburg
number one day occasions the gold breakfast
blue quilt, a Mexican girl talks at length
seagulls in a square garden lean into each
other on the surface horn's intaglio of happiness
sparkles the big gem of 24 hours

Descartes

1

Descartes came into the poem. He did not like his new job; the way the chairs, the hi-fi and the fire lean into each other. He came in, I have just cycled from Stockholm, there is a lot of road between there and here. Times Square had soured him, peeled off a few skins and measured the depth of green. It is as I thought, the valve worked loose outside Paris.

It's not as if he is Malherbe either, across the field the slant of December. Descartes couldn't give a toss for rounded edges like playing cards, a Roman resting place; a holloway, two on the way to work, the combined action of human and natural agents-like I said, he didn't notice these details. He changed my life, hat polish for a start and envy in the dark.

When he was tired, his mind elsewhere, tossing coconuts at the poet's lawn, anywhere but here, Descartes would sit and doze and fill the house with it. Brown, hairy, large. A fistful of encased piss milk, remember no memory, the mind elsewhere. The violated child, courage turn us now next the light through the leaves, this path can be traced to the Wiltshire border.

No, he would not take a walk but that dip down to the brook is the boundary of the two villages. Yes, you can go there, that's mine down to the brook. The horses of this complex geometry are curious as you go.

2

Is it raining at my back or silence
high in the end of day head Monday
waits on shiny hill the conceptual sun
rises on the circuit of new green spring

a quick look at the Dantean stars
window open, foxes yap if the moon is full
no animal sleeps silver bangs through
the heart the field fills with light

a short time now, the unseparate events
come together, Linda's paintings dry
in the last heat blue roots against a fire,
other plants an unfixed surface of blue
light   these are the forces of victory

3

the money is on the table
on the way out I was zipped up
dark and tight, I was Frank
O'Hara's orphan brother
planning a windy route
through the new green spring of air

the money is road signs, turn the hard U
in love is Shakespeare's cum sweet luv
I would kiss your mouth and the secret
deep in its flesh of everything said
or will you he said well I'm glad
you're pleased by something, walking
out of a Cl9 novel and upstairs at speed

*

de Kooning's face the chalk of March
on your tongue braille bird song, exciting
isn't it, he looked over the woman and
the room filled with light floats I thought
no that's not it where then 3 o'clock and
it's spring, a face like the sun in another room

*

You can tell it's dry the lawn's
cracking, we've got a wet axe here
a loose blade, lambswool hurts no one
he was behaving like that
the wood swelling into the head
an abstract movement, if it's language
that is the sun attendant warmth
            rising to meet it

Robin Hood

the hot symbolism of dawn rolls out
green and lush the air falls
over my head and onto my hands
the world pops up a 3D book

figures without obvious support,
there goes Robin Hood green like
the dawn the jolly mind
cross hatched with windows silver
trees and cars of the opposite row
sent spinning as day to day

there are different rooms where virtue
in a coat the colour of day
that's a nice coat, trust him
always the birds in the air
touch your face   the summer sky
fits like your favourite shirt

*

driving through the dread night of shire politics
rolling the sea swell and lunatic police cars
we have you John in our ears. Gloria, fruit
and carnival, carnival and sudden death

intention nouns its pleonastic way
"they must learn the principle of law and order"
her blonde pressure greens in the memory,
kiss me not her, one in the box the other raving
ah fuck it Frank, run from the madding crowd

Bach arranges the body about the instant of knowing
take a gun for example, an Italian apple
and the ocean of your cool hand
I held
          and would recommend to anyone

A Slogan Will Not Suffice

the work of the sun, not illusion
diamonds hidden in the kitchen calendar
we pin them in the cork and shiny frame
bills and visits and mathematical stars,
like a deck of marked cards.
you are already here,
the trial of love that should be love
each word against each word
                        down of your arm
I look, lift in my heart

trust the occasional radar through the dark,
the cold wheel cash holds together
it is a plot against the chickens of America
the wealth rolls off the Atlantic in neat symbols;
one dark raindrop, a semicircle of sunrays,
a pigeon wings it on hard blue March,
your money or your money and then
Spring comes with obscene practices in the sky
                        from every part of the ranch
the boys came to meet the new boss,
the man of style   I float my legs
in the bath of this weather.
She saws through the bread down to the table
slices each period of life is conducted
in the way life is conducted
and stores the table in the polar box for summer.
Eat strawberries and run away,
the lungs open the shoulder blades spread
and it smells like bread, like petals and horse shit
in the massed scents of May.

In the spring of cash R.A.F. boys probe the hills,
farmers in tractors bravely waving, our boys in dungarees
I walk in their film, you are in it, part of it.
Well captain, you look bitter, hurt and drunk.
I do? Yes. Well I am, just rub that for me and forget.
the trees scratch the fat sun
bad debts from the people we won't pay,
the postman said, silence in court the cat is pissing.

When I hear what it is meant to do to me
I hate it. I'd rather the flopped hollyhock
and yogurt lid, I'd rather the adverts
there is always music for your feelings, you are part of it,
like landscape in Thomas Hardy
under the heat of this traffic, beside yourself,
a man will leave if you fail, hello sir, it's me, Nic
on a horse taller than the hedge
he found a dead town formerly a zero
buzzed across the helloing girl
dark a girl garden decked in trees
families and traffic fresh from the word.

This is not Wittgenstein or a dream you could dream in sleep,
below the arrow of the town map outside the library,
You are here. The roads travel from the varnished frame
around pink blocks on bleached green
the whole thing looks nasty and fucked up;
the police station, the play-with-me-houses
and the insanitary schools.
I think of their real colour
the same sun greens the real town
I think of how we could have lived
I think five aces, hit the deck or die.

Printed in the United Kingdom
by Lightning Source UK Ltd.
107578UKS00001B/350